BOOKS BY
JAMES A. MICHENER

Tales of the South Pacific
The Fires of Spring
Return to Paradise
The Voice of Asia
The Bridges at Toko-Ri
Sayonara
The Floating World
The Bridge at Andau
Hawaii
Report of the County Chairman
Caravans
The Source
Iberia
Presidential Lottery
The Quality of Life
Kent State: What Happened and Why
The Drifters
A Michener Miscellany: 1950–1970
Centennial
Sports in America
Chesapeake
The Covenant
Space
Poland
Texas
Legacy
Alaska
Journey
Caribbean
The Eagle and the Raven
Pilgrimage
The Novel
The World Is My Home: A Memoir
James A. Michener's Writer's Handbook
Mexico
Creatures of the Kingdom
My Lost Mexico
Literary Reflections
Recessional
Miracle in Seville
This Noble Land: My Vision for America

with A. Grove Day
Rascals in Paradise

with John Kings
Six Days in Havana

This Noble Land

My Vision

for America

Random House • *New York*

James A. Michener

This Noble Land

My Vision for America

Library of Congress Cataloging-in-Publication Data

Michener, James A. (James Albert)
This noble land : my vision for America / James Michener.
p.   cm.
ISBN 0-679-45152-8
1. United States–Civilization–1970–   2. Social values–United
States.   I. Title.
E169.12.M497   1996
973.92–DC20   96-17912

Random House website address: http://www.randomhouse.com/

Printed in the United States of America on acid-free paper

24689753

FIRST EDITION

Book design by Carole Lowenstein

*This book is dedicated to
Random House's inspired editor
Kate Medina,
who first proposed this book to me
six years ago and who
kept encouraging me to write it.*

Acknowledgments

For the statistical research in this manuscript I am indebted to three young assistants who worked closely under my supervision. They are all from the University of Texas at Austin and are John Kings, my longtime assistant; Debbie Brothers, my equally longtime secretary; and Susan Dillon, who volunteered to join me as a research and computer expert. Their contributions occur on many pages in this book.

Contents

This
Noble
Land

My Vision
for America

One

My Qualifications for Judging My Homeland

*S*itting in my Texas garden as I approach my ninetieth birthday, I often reflect upon my life in the United States, enjoying what the nation offers now but shuddering at the pitfalls that threaten us in the years ahead. Since this report is an evaluation of life in my homeland, I had better begin with justifying why I consider myself qualified to brave making some judgments about America.

Foremost is my dedication to the United States. It began in the earliest years of my life. In a Presbyterian Sunday school I was taught that God had elected our country as His favorite land and all that our leaders did was in obedience to His loving care. Devoutly I believed that we were His special charges.

Each morning at our public school, which I attended from age six to eighteen, we opened the day with school prayer, the recitation of the Pledge of Allegiance and, on many mornings, the bellowing of a song that we sang in unison:

> 'O beautiful for spacious skies,
> For amber waves of grain,
> For purple mountain majesties
> Above the fruited plain!
> America! America!
> God shed His grace on thee

And crown thy good with brotherhood
From sea to shining sea!'

Each time I sang these words in my usual off-key voice, I was convinced that a universal brotherhood did exist in my noble homeland.

In those days the indoctrination of children with a love of their homeland began at age six and continued daily for the next twelve years. I have often thought back on that simpler time and concluded that it is better for a child to have some strong moral and social beliefs rather than none at all, even though his indoctrination may have been chauvinistic, muddled or even erroneous. Later he can correct error, but if he has allegiance to nothing he has nothing to work on in his later reeducation.

At an early age I began to know our country well, for at fourteen I hitchhiked north and south, and some years later I probed far to the west. In adult life I lived for extended periods in scattered states: Pennsylvania, Colorado, Massachusetts, New York, Hawaii, Maryland, Florida, Texas, Maine and Alaska. I spent shorter six-month periods in Virginia and Ohio, and I made enlightening visits of some length researching in the American islands of Samoa, Virgin Islands, Puerto Rico and Guam.

From these travels I acquired an appreciation of the fact that we are a country with unique blessings. Our land territory stretches from ocean to ocean, so we did not have to worry about our neighboring nations east or west; there were only those north and south, which, by great good fortune, were friendly nations: Canada and Mexico. True, we did have skirmishes with Canada, but we quickly backed off, and we did have far more serious wars with Mexico, from whom we acquired–or perhaps stole would be a better word–an amazingly rich southern tier of states that had belonged to her: Texas, New Mexico, Arizona, California, with extensions reaching into states like Colorado. But in general our neighbors' amicability allowed us freedom to develop peacefully inside our spacious borders. We owe much to Canada and Mexico.

Within our boundaries we have almost unimaginable riches: agricultural land capable of providing much of the rest of the world with wheat, corn, beef and other foods. We also have spectacular natural beauty: our vast prairies, our towering mountains, our deep canyons, our vital rivers. We are a land truly blessed, for beneath this beauty lie immense deposits of petroleum and the precious minerals gold and silver.

I established in seven of the big states what amounted to permanent homes and participated in the social, economic and political life of the areas. Thus I became familiar with eastern seaboard traditions, the radically different patterns in the Far West, the rigid values of New England, the seductive charm of the South, the unique character of life in Texas, the allure of Hawaii and the frozen wonders of Alaska, where I spent extended time one winter in total darkness north of the Arctic Circle. And on the islands–Pacific and Caribbean–I witnessed how our nation operated as a colonial power.

The reason I was deficient in my knowledge of the West Coast states was a somewhat complicated one. I married an American woman of Japanese descent, whose birth in the United States automatically made her an American citizen. But when we were catapulted into World War II by the Japanese sneak attack on Pearl Harbor, public opinion in California became so inflamed that my future wife's family was given two days to liquidate all their holdings and was moved into an American-style concentration camp that used the stables at the Santa Anita Racetrack as living quarters. In later years my wife boasted humorously: 'Our family occupied the stall of the great horse Equipoise.'

Despite her ability to make light of what had happened to her, she rebelled when I attempted in the 1960s to move our head-quarters to California so that I could write what I hoped would be a strong novel on that state. She said: 'I could not sleep easily in California. Remembering how they abused my mother and me would be too painful!' So I lost the opportunity to live in one of our mightiest states and write what might have been one of my better books.

However, in our later years she became forgiving: 'True, we were thrown into concentration camps, mine was in Colorado, but they must not be compared with Hitler's terrible death camps. None of us was killed or tortured, and last year the gov-ernment did compensate us for our losses—if only ten cents on the dollar—as a kind of apology for what they had done.' Then she laughed: 'By sending us to strange areas they forced us to leave what might later have developed into a Japanese ghetto in California. We scattered to places like New England, Utah, Okla-homa and, in my case, to a good life in Chicago, where I met you.'

I too would experience how difficult and sometimes cruel life in America can be, for I was born a foundling, reared in genteel poverty, and was occasionally brought to the local poorhouse when family funds diminished. My life till age fourteen was a struggle with deprivation, and when I had worked my way out of poverty—I was constantly employed from age eleven—I was faced by the Great Depression and the ravages of World War I.

I watched the brutal way in which American capitalism waged battle against labor unions and the tricks by which blacks were de-prived of their rights in the South. I also came out strongly against the death penalty, for I saw that it was imposed primarily upon the unfortunates in our society, seldom against the well-to-do, whose high-priced lawyers could be trusted to find a compassionate judge and a jury of middle-class conservatives to set them free.

But despite this early indoctrination into the uglier aspects of our political world, I was never attracted by the Communism then rampant. I was sensible enough to see that whereas some of its social principles were identical with some of mine, its economic proposals and its dictatorship had minimal chances of being adopted in the United States. My early conclusions on such matters never wavered and my rejection of state Communism became total.

As I matured I would write a series of comprehensive novels about my country, and in doing so, I had to immerse myself in research regarding Hawaii, Colorado, the Chesapeake lands, the American space program, Texas, Alaska and the Pennsylvania Dutch country. And when one has an in-depth understanding of the history of those varied areas, one almost automatically gains insight into what motivates our nation. I also wrote a protracted analysis of the sports world in America, as well as a little book, a kind of novel, that investigated the principles of our Constitution. During some of those years I also taught American history at various levels and made myself reasonably conversant with constitutional law.

From such experiences I gained a solid understanding of American history, economic development and social values. But I acquired even more instruction in the realities of American life during the five times in which I campaigned for one public office or another: electoral delegate for both Hubert Humphrey and Edmund Muskie; member of the U.S. House of Representatives—an unsuccessful but edifying bid; official of the Democratic Party; and, most important of all, delegate to and secretary for the splendid constitutional convention that rewrote the laws for the Commonwealth of Pennsylvania. I fought vigorously for various improvements in our state government: reduction of the ridiculous size of the legislature; merit appointment of judges; taxation on church property not used specifically for religious functions; and the elimination of superfluous row–office elective jobs like coroner and prothonotary. I lost every one of these battles, but when the convention ended, delegates from both parties appointed me to spend another six months helping to install the new governmental systems. I learned much about the United States from these excursions into the political realities. Specifically, I learned to admire the hardworking professional politicians in each party who labored diligently to make their party, their state and their nation a better place.

And finally, from these varied experiences I had just cause for believing that my land was indeed noble, a conviction from which I have never retreated. Consider how it treated me. After a bleak early period I was spotted as a lad able to learn and was encouraged to attend nine universities and centers of learning, including the incomparable Swarthmore and Harvard, and always at public expense. When I finished, I was eligible not only to pursue an enviable private career as a writer, but also to serve our nation as a naval officer (very junior grade) and as a member of some half–dozen government committees supervising the arts, the postal service, the space agency and the agencies both in Washington and Munich that were combating the Communism of the Soviet Union, a task in which I was engaged for many years.

I ended these adventures as a middle–class American who I think understood the problems of both the rich upper classes and those impoverished at the bottom. It is from such a background that I view my homeland as–I hope–a responsible and knowledgeable critic.

Two

Defining
a Noble
Land

When President Nixon wanted to appoint me to a board requiring a full-field loyalty check, the FBI reported that whereas I seemed to be a normal American citizen with no blemishes in my record, I had worked and lived abroad in a staggering number of foreign countries. The figure was somewhere in the seventies, and when I volunteered the names of other lesser locations they had understandably missed, the number came to a hundred and two. I had lived for substantial periods in Italy, Korea, Japan, Hungary, Austria, Afghanistan, Israel, Spain, South Africa, Poland, Canada, Mexico and the island groups in the South Pacific and the Caribbean.

In several of these countries I rented my residences, but I never acquired any real estate, although I was often tempted. I continued to pay my taxes in Pennsylvania and voted from there, even though in those years a writer, artist or actor could avoid taxes by taking residence abroad, especially in Ireland or Switzerland. I noticed, however, that the young men of my acquaintance who did so became severely disadvantaged. The writers and artists fell out of the mainstream of America; the actors were forced to accept mediocre parts in mediocre films shot on inadequate budgets in Italy and Spain. The émigrés saved a little money but paid a devastating penalty: the decline of their professional careers. I learned early that it was far more profitable to stay home, pay my taxes and march ahead with my contemporaries.

Nevertheless, I loved travel and went literally to all corners of the world, missing only a few choice places like Tibet, the South Pole and Machu Picchu in Peru. When I was eighty-five I finally made it to Antarctica and saw a world of wonders about which I had only dreamed, including vast icebergs, some as big as small villages. Through it all, I kept my emotional footing in the United States.

As I explored one country after another, I found myself saying repeatedly: 'I could live here very happily!' and I would some-times go so far as to identify specific spots that I would enjoy and in which I was sure I could do good work: a Swiss valley sur-rounded by the Alps, a ranch in Spain's Andalusia surrounded by gnarled olive trees, a fishing village on the Japanese seacoast, a remote lakefront in Canada, a woodland in Brazil, or a colorful English village south of London and convenient to the theaters and museums of my favorite city in the world.

But always I resisted the allurements, for I had developed a conviction that I needed to be home and was needed back there. I could never go into exile. Today I regret each heavenly spot I missed, but only as a sensible man feels about those dream girls he might have won had he tried.

While jumping from one major locale to another and seeing the very best of every country in which I worked–the most in-teresting villages, the most romantic natural settings and the most instructive people–I began formulating the following questions for evaluating the worth of a nation, and I continue to use them in my analyses and judgments of the nations of the world today. In the succeeding chapters I will evaluate our noble land in light of several of these questions, ones that concern what I believe are the most important services a nation should provide its citizens. Does the nation provide an equitable distribution of wealth? Equal treatment for all minorities? Good educational services? Adequate health care? Good performance in these criteria is an indication of a nation's ability to perform nobly.

Here are the questions I ask when assessing nations:

1. Has the nation been able to create a stable society?

I don't like police states, but I do want my society to be firmly rooted and devoted to the great traditions of the region. I want it to sponsor a climate in which the individual citizen can go to bed at night with reasonable assurance that when he rises the next morning his world will still be there, and next year, and forty years down the line when his children can take over with the same expectation of stability. Fundamental to every judgment I make is my strong desire to enjoy, improve and pass along a stable society. I would sacrifice much to ensure this.

I reached my conclusion on the importance of stability in society early in my studies of American history, for although I had the deepest respect for Thomas Jefferson and would surely have been one of his strongest supporters at the close of the eighteenth century, as the new century began I'm sure I would have equally appreciated the strong, no-nonsense conservatism in fiscal and governmental matters that Alexander Hamilton espoused. Even then I would have cherished the stability that he provided and without which no society can properly flourish. I have worked in a score of emerging nations in which life would have been so much better in most respects if there had been a local Alexander Hamilton.

A vital factor in the stability of a nation's society is the stability and strength of the society's basic unit, the family. I shall devote an entire chapter to a discussion of how the current deterioration in the traditional structure and strength of the American family is weakening the solidity of the entire nation.

2. Does the nation provide a reliable money system?

This is essential to the orderly progress of a nation. Individuals should have the right to expect that the money they save today will be of comparable value ten years later. Businesses can be strangled by wild fluctuations in currency.

But I am not so sure that the nation as a whole suffers too much from these fluctuations. I have watched explosive inflation in Germany and Brazil, and in a more limited sense in Japan, where I used to get 640 yen to one dollar, while now the rate is less than 100 to one. Nations, which coin and distribute their own money, can absorb such fluctuations, and I have begun to think that a sovereign nation cannot go bankrupt. The land is still there, so also are the people and the industries, and Japan and Germany have proved to the world that a nation can suffer brutal inflation and come roaring back much stronger than it was before. It is quite possible that the same might happen in America within twenty or thirty years.

But, of course, when such inflation strikes, it is the middle class of the population that suffers the most, and the lower and upper classes seem to survive with minimal damage. Since I am a member of the middle class, I shy away from those nations that cannot guarantee the stability of their currency.

3. Does the nation have a political system that ensures peaceful transitions of power from liberal to conservative and vice versa?

One of the glories of American and British government is the orderly way in which such transfers of power occur. In the United States we have an election on a Tuesday and by eleven o'clock that night the entire nation knows and accepts the fact that a new political power is now in charge. In nations like Italy and Israel, with their proliferation of fragmented political parties, sometimes no one knows who won an election for the two or three weeks required to sort out the electoral mess.

A concerned friend in Israel told me: 'We hold the election today and count the votes, without any conclusive result. So the real election begins tomorrow when the multiple various parties jockey for position. More often than you might think, some fringe fanatical party that won only three seats is able to dictate which of the major parties will take over, and then the entire nation is held at the mercy of those three votes. For God's sake, Mr. Michener, never allow proportional representation to gain a foothold in your country. That way lies disaster.'

From watching many such elections in Europe, I have grown to deplore proportional representation and the nurturing of marginal parties. They lead to indecision, make clear-cut programs practically impossible, and prevent society from initiating a bold change in direction under a clear winner who has been given a mandate to govern. The volatile nature of third-party movements like the Ross Perot phenomenon of 1992 makes us susceptible to the worst abuses of pluralism and proportionalism.

I appreciate the system in New Zealand, where liberals and conservatives alternate with surprising frequency. At the start of any campaign in which one party is likely to oust the other, this is one of the first pledges made and honored: 'We will preserve every good law our opponents have passed. What we'll do is administer them more effectively.' And power changes hands amicably, the hallmark of an effective political system.

I am aware that frequently in American history the brilliant philosophers of some third party have championed sensible improvements in government, improvements that the two major parties have been wise enough to appropriate. Opening the eyes and hearts of the major parties might be the acceptable role of the third party. I can live with such a system, provided that the third party is not awarded an assured portion of the electoral vote.

4. Does the nation provide its citizens, especially the young, with adequate health services?

The events in the United States in recent years have shown how volatile this issue is and how far we are from a reasonable solution (I shall discuss this essential factor more fully later). In the meantime we are the world's only major nation without a health system that protects everyone. The recent flood of persuasive ads in which doctors and nurses state that 'America has the best system of health care in the world' prompts the cynic to ask: 'For whom?'

And just as society should hold itself responsible for giving a child a healthy start in life, so also should it provide some easy and honorable way to ease the ending of a person's life. I do not mean the support only of nursing homes or retirement areas with nursing facilities; I mean the structuring of an entire society so that medical services and continued and loving care are kept available. I do not advocate any form of euthanasia, but I firmly believe that states should pass legislation making the thoughtful use of living wills available and operative. No patient should be obligated to undergo prolonged heroic measures to save his or her life when that life has deteriorated to the point when it is no longer meaningful.

5. Does the nation provide effective schools, colleges, universities and schools for industrial training?

I shall also discuss this question of education more fully later; education is so important that every year I live I give it increased weight in my judging system. Put simply, a nation that allows its schools to become ineffective dooms itself to a secondary position when competing with the workforces of other nations, such as Japan and Germany, that have not only maintained educational standards but improved them. An effective school system is a preeminent obligation for any society; children have enormous potential that can never be brought into effective use without the most careful and persistent training. The son of a Neanderthal family had to learn to make arrowheads and trail wild animals. And for the child born in America today it is essential that he master the computer.

6. Does the nation provide free libraries?

Of vital importance is whether the nation provides free libraries at which adults can continue to educate themselves after graduation or to help them educate themselves if they have not finished school or college. I shudder whenever I hear that a community has closed its library. With the revolutionary changes occurring in our workforce, and with radically new demands being made by potential employers, the people young and old who do not continue educating themselves run the risk of becoming unemployed or unemployable. 'Learn and earn' could well become the mantra for the oncoming generations in all the nations of the world and especially in the United States.

7. Does the nation provide adequate employment opportunities for the young person as he or she approaches adulthood?

Obtaining a first job is a crucial step in the maturation of a teenager who has just left high school or a young man or woman who has been graduated from college. The leap into adult citizenry starts with a job. Young people must not be deprived of the vital opportunity of working for a living, of actually supporting themselves and perhaps a family and of becoming contributors to the nation's wealth as well as consumers of it. The Ph.D. scholar who cannot find employment can become a social menace; any young person who is denied work and a living wage can become a walking time bomb.

It is the responsibility of a nation to provide employment for its young. The question of whether a nation enables its young to become producers and thus contributors to the nation's wealth will be a major focus of this book.

8. Does the nation provide a financial/taxation system that helps keep the difference between the very rich and the very poor at an acceptable level, and does it encourage the development of a moderately well-to-do middle class of entrepreneurs?

I deem this to be one of the crucial responsibilities of a society and I am appalled at nations like Mexico that generate considerable wealth but refuse to distribute it up and down the economic ladder. The failure to develop a sturdy middle class is a sign of weakness, one that condemns a society to mediocrity at best and revolution at worst. I will elaborate later on my contention that the United States has grown sloppy in dealing with this problem of the distribution of wealth and must try to redress the imbalance.

9. Does the nation provide churches for the moral guidance of its people and especially its leaders?

I believe that a society requires moral values and a conviction to abide by them. History is replete with examples of strong-minded citizens who have acquired a solid moral foundation without the assistance of organized religion–churches or priests or rabbis–but it is risky for the nation as a whole to rely on the chance that its citizens will individually apply themselves to building a stable moral base without benefit of organized religion. It is better to enlist the churches in providing moral instruction, even indoctrination, for the vast majority of its young people. I have found that a man without strong moral principles is like a ship without a rudder; he cannot be depended upon to remain upright in a storm. I would never want to live in a community that did not have influential churches.

10. Does the society provide recreational opportunities?

In my studies of world cultures, I have been constantly impressed to see that each seminal culture sponsored athletic contests for the amusement of the public and for competition between states. It can be no accident that Greece and Rome had centers for competition, and that Saint Paul would refer several times to the athletic games of his new Christians. Historians repeatedly mention hippodromes for racing, arenas for boxing and other diversions, and fields for horsemanship. Vigorous athletic participation is as old as civilization and must therefore be fulfilling a basic need.

However, the nation cannot allow legitimate athletic competition to degenerate into brutal violence that glorifies the often destructive macho aspects of human nature. Unfortunately, in the United States the growing violence in sports has become part and parcel of a growing acceptance of violence as a normal factor in the life of our society. I shall discuss at length how this glorification of macho behavior in our society is damaging the traditions upon which we founded and built our nation.

11. Does the society provide access to museums, opera houses, symphony halls, theaters, parks and zoos?

At the same time that the ancients were promoting athletic competitions, they seem to have spent just as much of their resources on theaters for the presentation of plays, stages for mime and dance, and on structures adorned with majestic sculptures and fine paintings. I admire good athletic competition, but I love music, the theater, dance, sculpture and painting; they form the benchmark by which cultures are judged. Sports and the arts must be kept in balance.

While I grant that perhaps even a majority of citizens would express little interest in 'cultural' functions and would be loath to

support them, I believe they are essential to a good public life–
they are not only for the pleasure of the upper classes or the cultural elite. Mankind's more esoteric achievements should also be
made available to underprivileged children, a random few of
whom will develop an interest in art or in opera. As I did–that
was my history; the availability of good libraries, art museums
and great symphony halls meant that I could educate myself, regardless of whether or not I had instructors. This kind of self-
education should be made possible for all young people, and if
they ignore the opportunities it will be to their loss. The boy or
girl who discovers the world's intellectual treasures becomes
open to endless adventures and self-improvement.

Cultural institutions should be supported with tax money, if
possible. I am personally willing to help support my country's
cultural organizations through taxation because I have little regard for any society that refuses to assist such institutions financially. I told one group of city leaders who were debating whether
they could afford a new stadium: 'Any city is a collection of citizens who *behave* like a city. That means they are obligated to provide a stadium for sports, a theater for drama and dance and
opera, an art museum, and a very strong chain of free libraries.'
That's what cities are all about, and nations, too.

*12. Is the nation able to balance the different cultural and ethnic and racial
groups within its society, and does it treat all such groups equitably?*

I believe that in the United States the deterioration of racial relations has become so intense that there is a risk of interracial
strife unless the situation is drastically improved. No nation can
allow its social, political or economic systems to discriminate
against any one segment of its society. Neither can it allow minorities to become so frustrated that they feel it is futile to try to
educate themselves or to raise their standards of living.

13. Does the nation provide an orderly system whereby the interests of the aged are protected from the ravages that overtake them?

I place a high priority on this social obligation primarily, I suppose, because I am myself subject to the demands and realize how delinquent we are as a society in caring for our older people. Compared with nations that have a superior social concern about the welfare of the aged—China, Japan, Denmark, Sweden, Korea and the smaller East Asian countries—we are far behind and ought to make a serious effort to catch up.

In my travels I have constantly applied these criteria to other countries as well as to my own, and found that differences between societies are glaring; not surprisingly, I have concluded that certain societies are more admirable than others. To deny this is to blind oneself to reality. At the end of six decades of persistent evaluation of nations I am prepared to present some conclusions as to how the United States compares with other nations.

Evaluations

CHARACTERISTIC	HISTORICAL U.S.	CONDITION TODAY
Stable society	Superb, up to now	But imperiled by racial conflict in decades ahead.
Reliable money system	Superior, up to now	But within the near future heavy debt poses a fearful danger.
Orderly political change	Impeccable so far	But the threat of third parties is real and ominous.
Adequate health services	Low average among leading nations	Far behind Canada, Great Britain, Germany, Scandinavia in making care available and affordable.

Educational system	Grades 1 to 6 fine; high school deplorable; college low average; graduate studies superior	Behind France, Germany, Japan, Scandinavia in providing mastery of fundamentals.
Free libraries	Has been world's best, still good	But grievously endangered by budget cuts and closing of branches.
Employment opportunities	Has been superior	Bad slippage recently. Lags behind Japan, Germany, China.
Distribution of wealth	Superior in making a well-to-do middle class possible	Distance between very wealthy and very poor is deplorable. Also, middle class suffers.
Churches	Exceptional	But reactionary drift threatens future political stability.
Recreation opportunities	Superior, as of now	But raw commercialism endangers sports system.
Higher cultures	Excellent so far	But entire structure endangered by budget cuts and attacks.
Racial equality	Poor in the past	Becoming worse.
Care for the aged	Historically delinquent, and even now lagging behind most countries	Social systems of China, Japan, Scandinavia far ahead.

A quick scan of the middle column above will explain why I feel justified in describing my homeland as a great society, especially during the decades of my growing up. Except for the racial discrimination that has been our national disgrace throughout our history, we excelled in so many important categories and reached respectable levels even in those where other nations surpassed us that I had a right to be proud.

As I now review the column I begin to wonder if my favorable evaluation of America was skewed by the intense indoctrination I received from my first day in Sunday school and, more important, my first morning in public school. For the first six or seven years of my education I lapped up patriotism until I acquired a faith in my country that has never since diminished. It continues to dictate my behavior at unexpected times and provides me with an almost automatic set of responses when public values are being challenged. I am not wise enough to determine whether that early and incessant indoctrination made me too uncritical.

But a study of the third column proves that today I am able to see American society with a more critical eye. I stand by every evaluation in that column and might make some of the judgments even harsher.

What the plethora of negative evaluations in the summary suggests is that our society is in danger, and, in some cases like the failure of large parts of our educational system, even in peril. The magnitude of these fracture points and what can be done to anticipate and escape them will be the focus of the remaining chapters in this essay.

Three

The Distribution of America's Wealth

I have been privileged to know American families at almost every level of income, from the Texas oil billionaires, about whom I have written, to the numerous garden-variety rich families with not much over a million. A large proportion of the families with which I have worked fall into the huge middle class with salaries around $75,000, and because I work with students I know scores who live on less than $10,000 a year. In the years prior to World War II the highest salary I ever had was $4,800 a year, so that a salary of $75,000 was far beyond the limits of my imagination, but of course $4,800 in the thirties was worth many times more than it is worth today. I have also been keenly interested in the street people so common in our cities who have minimal income and often no place to call home. They are outcasts, and I have never understood how they could have reached that appalling level. I cannot comprehend how a healthy man in his forties can have wasted his life and ended in the gutter, but even more incomprehensible is how a mother with two children could land beside him.

From a study of people with various levels of income I have come to realize just how important a living wage is. Fundamental to every problem I discuss in this book is not only our nation's wealth but how it is distributed among the citizens.

So that we can have figures to refer to in our discussion, I present two different charts: the first listing outstanding family accumulations of wealth sometimes dating back to the last century; the second showing yearly incomes of a random selection of people living today.

For *Forbes* magazine in 1994, $350 million marked the cutoff point between the very wealthy on the one hand and the merely elite who are categorized as 'the comfortable millionaires.' The 'moderately wealthy' trail behind in their $100 million ghettos.

In April 1995 *The New York Times* reported that Federal Reserve figures from 1989, which the paper said were the most recent numbers available, revealed that 'the wealthiest 1% of American households–with net worth of at least $2.3 million each–[owned] nearly 40% of the nation's wealth. . . . Farther down the scale, the top 20% of Americans–households worth $180,000 or more–[possess] more than 80% of the country's wealth.' A year later, in April 1996, *The Wall Street Journal* reported that an analysis by the New York compensation consultants Pearl Meyer & Partners Inc. done for the newspaper showed that 'the heads of about 30 major companies received compensation that was 212 times higher than the pay of the average American employee.'

Here is a list of some of the country's wealthiest families:

Family Fortunes Accumulated in the Past but Still Intact (a sampling)

NAME	YEAR	SOURCE	TOTAL
Walton family	1995	Wal-Mart stores	$23.45 billion
Gates III, William	1995	Microsoft	$12.89 billion
Buffett, Warren	1995	Stocks	$10.68 billion
du Pont family	1995	Du Pont Co.	$10 billion
Newhouse brothers	1995	Publishing	$8 billion
Mars family	1995	Candy	$7.5 billion
Rockefeller family	1995	Oil	$6 billion
Bass family	1995	Oil	$5.73 billion
Allen, Paul	1995	Microsoft	$5.3 billion

Mellon family	1995	Banking	$5 billion
Perelman, Ronald	1995	Leveraged buyouts	$4.69 billion
Hearst family	1995	Newspapers	$4.5 billion
Lauder, Estée, and sons	1995	Cosmetics	$3 billion
Tisch brothers	1995	Loews Corp.	$2.8 billion
Perot, Ross	1995	Computer services	$2.5 billion
Ford family	1995	Ford Motor Co.	$2 billion
Kroc, Joan	1995	McDonald's	$1.74 billion
Turner, Ted	1995	TBS Inc.	$1.72 billion
Wrigley family	1995	Chewing gum	$1.45 billion
Busch family	1995	Anheuser–Busch	$1.4 billion
Marriott family	1995	Hotels	$1.39 billion
Disney family	1994	Walt Disney Co.	$840 million
Copley, Helen	1994	Publishing	$575 million
Kohler family	1994	Plumbing fixtures	$550 million
Coors family	1994	Beer	$400 million
Kennedy family	1994	Stocks	$350 million

Sources: *Forbes, Fortune,* various news articles

The implications of the concentration of wealth into few hands are enormous. Kevin Phillips, a conservative Republican columnist, whose 1990 book, *The Politics of Rich and Poor,* is a bible on this theme, aptly sums up the effect upon our nation of this growing accumulation of wealth at the top:

> It is not enough to describe the United States as the world's richest nation between 1945 and 1989. The distribution of its wealth conveys a more provocative message. By several measurements, the United States in the late twentieth century led all other major industrial countries in the gap dividing the upper fifth of the population from the lower–in the disparity between top and bottom.

Several observations should be quickly made. The conspicuous fortunes like the Rockefellers', the Fords', the Carnegies' and the Dewitt Wallaces' have been converted into great trusts whose yearly interest on their investments is applied to the public good. The money has not been wasted, and many other families in this elite group have established their own foundations with equally commendable purposes but with smaller initial funding. Unfortunately, other possessors of large fortunes have been social parasites, contributing little but their income taxes, while still others–the Bill Gateses and the Paul Allens, for example–have so recently emerged that we cannot guess what directions they will take when their period of accumulation has ended.

From time to time I shall consider historical precedents that throw light upon our situation, and few of these will be more illustrative than an overview of what happened in several earlier societies when the ownership of wealth became dangerously unbalanced. One such period, when stupendous fortunes were concentrated in a few hands, occurred in the medieval era when all Europe and some of northern Africa was unified in one dominant religion. The Catholic Church proliferated with its Roman and Orthodox branches and was extremely wealthy. To increase its riches the Church's officials paid special attention to older men and women of wealth, especially well-to-do widows. As these Christians approached death the Church applied heavy pressure on them to will to the Church their money, their art holdings and especially the vast lands they had acquired.

Many of these wealthy old patrons succumbed to the Church's blandishments and willed all their holdings to the nearby monasteries or convents, so that over time the religious orders became the custodians of a large percentage of the society's wealth. This transfer of money, art and material wealth other than land did little damage to the general economy, but it did create envy and animosity among the kings, nobles and lesser rulers, who saw that what might otherwise have come to them had instead been acquired by the Church.

Real harm to the general welfare of the countryside did occur, however, with the transfer of land to the Church because it withdrew huge tracts from the peasants who had fed their families from crops grown on land they had for generations considered their own. Even though they had not owned the land, they felt themselves entitled to continued occupancy. Once the lands came under the control of the Church, however, the peasants learned they would no longer be allowed to control any of the produce of the lands they tilled. All produce entered the marketplace under the ownership of the Church, which grew richer while the poor grew poorer.

This appallingly negative process became known as *Le Mortmain de l'Église*, the dead hand of the Church. By retaining both the land and all of its produce for its own profit, the Church disrupted the traditional customs of merchandising. It converted the once semifree peasants into serfs, who now had to buy the produce they themselves had raised. Some trivial economic benefit did result from this transfer of land to the Church, for monks proved to be able custodians, but the benefits were far less than what a diligent peasantry controlling the produce from its own fields or from the fields of its masters could have produced.

In the fourteenth and fifteenth centuries this dead hand of the Church became so oppressive that rumors of rebellion began to circulate, and in the opening years of the sixteenth century dramatic events unfolded in various parts of Europe that would modify the history of the world. In England, King Henry VIII began his stormy involvement with a succession of six wives by divorcing his first, Catherine of Aragon, and beheading two of her successors. To win his divorce Henry had to defy both the religious strictures against divorce and the dictates that the pope thundered at him from Rome. In surprisingly quick order Henry showed himself strong enough to ignore the pope and to lead the

Catholic Church in England into open rebellion against papal authority. While remaining outwardly Catholic, the English Church sowed the seed that would end in its becoming a Church of its own, the established Church of England.

Having accomplished what at the time must have seemed a miracle, for the Catholic Church of Rome was all-powerful, Henry broadened his campaign against the pope by ordering that all the monasteries and convents in England be dissolved, the monks and nuns thrown out into the countryside, and the ownership of Church lands transferred to local knights and barons to ensure their loyalty to the Crown. The dead hand of the Church was thus transformed into the bold hand of the barons. The lot of the peasants attached to the land was not conspicuously improved; nor were the agricultural practices. But a vast revolutionary change had swept England: a new Church, a new landownership, a new spirit of defiance. A cynic has accurately summarized the peaceful revolution: 'So Protestantism in England was born of concupiscence and cupidity.'

There is no evidence that Henry engineered his break from Rome with any avowed intention of transferring Church property to the barons, but that is what happened. Nor did he intend to convert the serfs of the Church into semifreemen responsible to local English landlords, but that also happened. It was a revolution of enormous significance, which started with a divorce proceeding and ended in a fundamental change in landownership.

Meanwhile, in Germany, a stubborn monk, Martin Luther, was launching his own rebellion against papal authority. Initially, his was a clean-cut philosophical rebellion, which, from the start, presaged an eventual break with Rome and the establishment of a new denomination, Lutheranism, although he never called it that. (Toward the close of his rebellion, sex played a role much as it had with Henry VIII; Luther enticed the nun Katharina von Bora to leave her convent by renouncing her vows and to marry him.)

Luther's plans initially contained nothing parallel to the disso-
lution of the English monasteries; indeed, when revolutionary
German peasants tried to wrest lands from the Church, Luther
sided with the Church and against the peasants. He wanted no
physical uprisings in Germany, merely the ecclesiastical reorder-
ing of Church procedures and freedom from the domination of
the monks, who had been so oppressive and in many instances
totally inept.

Eventually, following the revolutions in theology begun by
Luther, movements did occur to divest the monasteries of their
vast landholdings, and the results were similar to those in England: the newly freed lands fell into the hands of the nobility
while the serfs profited little.

Within a relatively few decades, these two rebellious denomi-
nations reshaped the history of modern Europe: an independent
Church of England only slightly removed, in ritual, from Rome;
and lusty Lutheranism, whose principles would become manifest
in various nations, each under its own charismatic leadership:
Ulrich Zwingli in Switzerland, John Knox in Scotland, and especially John Calvin in scattered localities throughout Europe.

In the parts of continental Europe where the Protestant revolutions did not take hold, neither did the revolution in landownership occur, and vast landholdings remained concentrated
either in the monasteries or with seminoble patrons. These lands
were called latifundia in Spain, in eastern Europe and, in time, in
the New World countries. I was on the scene in several countries
when some of the latifundia were broken up and tillable lands
distributed to the peasants–it occurred in Mexico when I worked
there–but even today in some nations in Latin America, such as
Argentina, and in certain parts of eastern Europe the great estates
remain undivided.

Why is the situation of medieval Europe applicable to our situation today in the United States? Certainly vast Church hold-

ings never became an aspect of our land management. Indeed, in 1862 during our Civil War, our Congress passed three extraordinary acts that literally gave away to private farmers and others the latifundia that our nation had accumulated. The Homestead Act gave worthy settlers free farmland; the Morrill Act set aside huge tracts of good land to finance agricultural colleges that charged minimal or even no student fees; and, in the same years, Congress quietly gave to the railways that had been inching their way westward enormous grants of free land to be used by them to encourage settlement in the West. I judge these three laws to have been among the wisest ever passed by our Congress, and I believe they helped us to avoid the radical solutions to landownership that so frequently tore Europe apart.

But did we completely escape problems similar to those created by *Le Mortmain de l'Église?* Not at all. Our indecent concentrations of power have occurred not in landownership but in the ownership of other forms of our nation's tangible wealth. In the 1520s England and Germany faced revolution of one kind or another; now, nearly five hundred years later, the United States is heading down the path toward its own version of revolution.

As American wealth has been accumulating in fewer pockets, the salaried workers of the huge middle class have watched their incomes remain static or even decline. The bottom third of society has slid ever closer to the poverty level, while those already in poverty have found no way to work themselves out of it. In the 1980s legal government policies were established with but one apparent objective: to enable the rich to grow even richer while the poor were pushed to ever-lower rungs on the economic ladder. The 1980s were a decade of shame.

The figures of inherited and accumulated wealth that I listed at the beginning of this chapter are interesting and indicative of a major problem in our society, but even more meaningful to the average observer are the grotesque amounts of yearly income being acquired today by many of our nation's new millionaires. A small sampling of these includes:

Contemporary Yearly Income, Including in Some Cases Bonuses and Stock Options

NAME	YEAR CITED	SOURCE	CASH INCOME
Milken, Michael	1987	Junk bonds	$550 million
Eisner, Michael	1993	Disney Co.	$203 million
Spielberg, Steven	1994	Film	$165 million
Winfrey, Oprah	1995	TV	$74 million
Streisand, Barbra	1994	Music, film	$52 million
Jackson, Michael	1995	Music	$45 million
Cosby, Bill	1994	Entertainment	$34 million
Jordan, Michael	1994	Basketball, baseball	$30.01 million
King, Stephen	1995	Writing	$22 million
Houston, Whitney	1993	Music, film	$18 million
Limbaugh, Rush	1993	TV, writing	$15 million
Goizueta, Roberto	1993	Coca-Cola	$14.5 million
Montana, Joe	1994	Football	$10.3 million

Contrast the above incomes with:

A married working couple	1994	Lawyer, manager	$98,280
Blue-collar worker	1994	Fast-food counterman	$10,608

Sources: *Forbes, Fortune,* newspapers, government data

There is a vast psychological difference between the first table, which shows accumulated wealth and inherited fortunes, and this small sampling of contemporary yearly incomes. Many of the names in the first list are those of historic figures who accu- mulated their fortunes in the distant past. The modern citizen does not envy them their good fortune; it happened so long ago and there is nothing we can do about it.

But the names in the second list are our contemporaries. Many could be the man or woman next door, some of them relatively young, and their excessive incomes become a matter of moment. Although we can see lasting proof of the socially desirable ways in which many of the past inheritors of great wealth converted their money into commendable foundations, we have little proof as to how these newly rich will distribute theirs. We catch fleeting glimpses of this or that celebrity's making a gift to a school or to a movement that has social merit, but even these relative pittances are offset by the appalling illustrations of opulent decadence, such as the dream house young Bill Gates is building in the Seattle area for himself and his bride. With forty thousand square feet of living space at a cost of some $30 million, it goes far beyond Thorstein Veblen's notion of conspicuous consumption.

But if thoughtful Americans do not waste time envying the recipients of great wealth, they are obligated to consider the evils that ensue when a nation's wealth is distributed with cruel unfairness. In late June 1996 a study group at the University of Michigan, which has been conducting an ongoing analysis of how the wealth of America is distributed, released data proving conclusively that the rich families in America were indeed getting richer by the hour, while the people at the bottom of the economic ladder remained in dire poverty. More specifically, as reported by *The New York Times*, the Michigan data found that 'The most prosperous 10 percent of American households held 61.1 percent of the nation's wealth in 1989 and 66.8 percent in late 1994.' Just two days before the Michigan figures were announced, the Census Bureau released its own study of the same phenomena, confirming that there is an ever-widening disparity between the rich and other segments of society.

My own prediction based on the Michigan data is that year by year the discrepancy between rich and poor will grow wider until finally it will become intolerable. If my extrapolations are correct, I would expect that some time in the next century something will snap and there will be a violent upheaval. The grossly unequal distribution of wealth is felt most brutally in the family incomes of the very poor. The government's 1993 definition of the poverty level for a family of three is a family income of less than $11,522 a year; in the United States in that year 15.1 percent of the nation's population fell below the official government poverty level. Only government intervention in the form of food stamps, rental allowances and aid for the children of deprived families enabled these very poor to continue to function even at a very low level.

The plight of our poor today is similar to what the dispossessed suffered in medieval Europe or what they experienced in Dickensian Britain a century and a half ago. We have made some progress in caring for our poor, but not nearly what a great industrial nation should have achieved.

Forbes magazine, in its issue of November 21, 1994, revealed a nasty secret about how some of the very rich handle their wealth. The magazine listed six American multibillionaires by name and business affiliation who had discovered a clever trick for avoiding taxes on the yearly income from their investments. A billion dollars prudently invested can yield many millions of income every year without invading the principal. According to *Forbes*, these six billionaires, who were named and photographed by *Forbes*, simply left the United States, legally renouncing their American citizenship, and enjoyed millions of dollars of tax-free income. The story was also picked up by *The New York Times* and *The Wall Street Journal*.

Most conspicuous among the expatriates identified by *Forbes* was young John T. Dorrance III, scion of the Campbell Soup Company, who resides in Ireland. The Campbell heir's fortune is similar to that of the Ford family's in that both fortunes were acquired by providing the nation with a much-sought-after commodity–in Ford's case a reasonably priced automobile, in Campbell's a good canned soup that quickly established itself as a best buy in the marketplace. But there the similarity ends because Ford's family used much of its fortune to endow a major foundation that has sponsored many worthwhile charities and studies of American life, whereas, although Campbell Soup also has a foundation, a Campbell heir has opted, according to Forbes, to leave the country that sustained him to take advantage of tax alternatives available out of the country. (A Campbell spokesperson didn't have an official confirmation of Mr. Dorrance's citizenship, but did say in June 1996 that Mr. Dorrance's 'official residence is outside the United States, in Ireland.')

Self-expatriation to avoid U.S. taxes on fortunes earned in the United States widens the gap between rich and poor, and sends a dangerous message to the less affluent, who often feel heavily burdened by the taxes they conscientiously pay. Such an action is so offensive that I find it difficult to express the full extent of my condemnation.

Once the tax-avoidance loophole became apparent, our government proposed a new tax that would eliminate the advantages enjoyed by the expatriates, but powerful lobbyists rushed in to protect the billionaires. They claimed that the proposed tax might disrupt ordinary trade relations between nations, it might discourage foreign persons from investing in American businesses, it might involve double taxation, and so on. But the underlying thread of all this was the assumption that it would be unfair to the billionaires who had worked hard to amass their wealth. Action on the proposed new law was delayed; a year later, a couple of versions are still pending, and the largess to the already rich continues. No comparable concessions have been made to the middle or lower classes.

Everyone has an opinion about taxes, and mine is based on long and bewildering experience. When I filed my last yearly report the paperwork required forty-eight pages of computations–I had a modest income from numerous foreign countries, all with different rules–and of this blizzard of figures I could understand only about the first three pages. It is preposterous that a national tax program should be so complicated that even an individual with an advanced college degree has no chance whatever of filing his own tax return and therefore has to hire an accountant.

I have often daydreamed about an easier system in which I could list at the end of the year every penny I'd earned and then pay a clearly defined and understandable tax–no deductions, no tax-evasion gambits, no chicanery, no accountants. I supposed that would never happen, because it was too sensible, too easy, and allowed no room for Congress to tuck into tax law little goodies for their constituents. But now I find that leaders in Congress are seriously considering what has been termed a flat tax, which is almost the same as what I had dreamed of. Proponents make intelligent defenses of such a tax, and others refine it a bit by introducing three or four levels of taxation, each level of income being taxed more than the level below. Thus the poor might pay nothing, the next level a minimum, and each step upward a little more. The top level would not be confiscatory. I decided that I preferred the simple flat tax, no gradations.

But as soon as I elected that system, financial counselors put forth a score of reasons why it either would not work or would be unfair to many levels if it did work. I was left bewildered, but either version of a flat or near-flat tax would be preferable to what I live with today.

However, the flat tax does nothing to alleviate the differences between rich and poor; indeed, the versions I've heard about leave the poor where they were but award the already rich with substantial benefits and, in many cases, lower taxes. Unless the proposed systems rectify this imbalance I would not be able to support them.

Looking carefully at the distress of the very poor and the severe financial discomfort of many in the middle class, I regretfully conclude that these imbalances in income will continue in American life indefinitely. But we shall have to alleviate the problem one way or another.

The United States can feed itself and much of the rest of the world using much less than 60 percent of our present farm workforce. And our manufacturing genius can, with no more than 60 percent of our present factory workers, provide all the consumer goods we need. This means that we will have a permanently unemployed mass of working men and women—a situation we're facing right now.

The strategic problem becomes: How can we pump into the lowest 15 percent or 20 percent of our idle population enough spending money so that they can function as economic units in our complicated system? I want to place money into their hands not only to help them but also to aid the rest of us. It is imperative that the very poor remain part of our economic system, spending what money they have in our stores, but for them to play this essential role they must somehow acquire money.

For many years I have pondered this almost insoluble problem, and no reasonable solution seems practical. I lived in Great Britain in the 1930s when much of that nation was on the dole, a solution that gave the unemployed poor a cash allowance. While

the dole was effective in achieving what I deem a major good–
the spreading around of money that could enter the economic
bloodstream in an orderly fashion–I deplored the demoralizing
effect the solution had on its recipients. I knew there must be a
better way, but I was unable to define it then, and even now, sixty
years later, I cannot think of a better way to support the unemployed, and neither can our nation's leaders. I would certainly regret seeing a gratis dole–that is, the indiscriminate distribution of
unearned money–established in our country. But I need not
worry–the general public would not allow it.

In the United States I witnessed the operation of the Works
Progress Administration, under President Franklin Roosevelt,
which contained too many negative aspects to be effective. A
major cause of its failure was that our labor unions would not
allow the government to institute serious or effective work programs lest jobs be taken away from union workers.

I was more favorably impressed by the Civilian Conservation
Corps, which had, so far as I could see, a faultless program in
which young people could do constructive work for their communities while earning a modest salary. I would have hopes for
such a program, were one to be reinstituted now.

I was enthusiastic about the National Youth Administration,
which encouraged young people to go to college or to remain
there if already enrolled. Helping to supervise its program in Colorado, I was authorized to help as fine a group of young people
as I would ever know: each receiving the munificent sum of $35
a month, they assisted our college by working in the library,
policing the campus, helping the local public schools as assistant
teachers or performing a wealth of other useful tasks.

It was an admirable gesture for our federal government to
make, but it exacted a personal penalty. Professors at the college
complained that three of my recipients were not performing

well at their assigned tasks or in their studies. When I looked into the matter I found the complaints to be justified. The cause was simple. These three young scholars were sending to their impoverished parents out on the Colorado dry lands, where the Depression was cruel, half the money I gave them for their own upkeep. These admirable young people were living on $17.50 a month and were starving themselves. In some cases I made up the difference from my own pocket, for I knew that we were all in this together.

My knowledge of history warns me that if, like the medieval church, we allow great wealth to accumulate in a few hands, and if we continue to allow the rich to become richer while greater numbers of the middle class slide into near poverty and the poor grow ever more desperate, revolution of some kind will become inevitable. In the United States it may be long deferred, for we are still a rich and powerful land that can absorb some errors, but the potential for violence cannot be ignored. I am deeply worried about our unwillingness to face up to this crucial problem of how to get spending money into the hands of the lower third of our population.

Recommendations

1. We should immediately abandon our juvenile faith in the trickle-down theory, which preaches that if you structure your tax system so that a few fortunate people can grow very rich, out of the goodness of their hearts they will allow some of their wealth to trickle down to those less fortunate below. A favorite justification for such a theory is that a rising tide lifts all the boats in the bay, which is a reassuring thought unless the smallest boats have already been swamped and sunk with no possibility

of being afloat again. Our government must stop passing income tax laws and other laws whose only purpose is to siphon even more wealth into the hands of those already rich while penalizing those at the lower end of the economic scale.

2. We must remind our more affluent citizens that taxes are the contribution they must make to prevent revolution from below. A major function of government is to provide a workplace in which its citizens can earn at least living wages, and then the government must tax them sensibly to pay for the social services, the police, the hospitals, the schools and the libraries and other benefits.

3. Our brightest economic minds must address themselves to the difficult technical problem of how we can best get money into the hands of the poor. I doubt that we shall see again a growing economy that can provide a place for all workers. We are faced with a body of permanent unemployables.

4. But we must also do everything possible to bring the able unemployed back into a revised form of our workforce. We must create jobs that can be performed by undereducated people.

5. I think we must also restudy the problem of our national debt, which we are told will impose a fearful burden on our grandchildren, and political leaders issue dire warnings about the destructive influence of a trillion-dollar debt. But debt is the stake a government manipulates to attain worthy ends. For example, in the crucial years of the 1500s, when the Spanish Armada threatened to destroy England, the difference between France and England was that the former was fiscally conservative and refused to add to its debt to keep up with England, while the latter incurred enormous debt to build a war fleet, to send explorers and settlers to the new worlds being discovered and to develop the industries

and banking systems that would support the great adventures. Improperly handled, debt can lead to disaster and the devaluation of currency. But properly managed, it ensures future growth and achievement. I am in favor of a reasonable debt and would not agree that present–day operations be strangled to achieve a pleasant–sounding 'reduction of the debt to zero.' The values that accrue to that philosophy are apt to prove illusory.

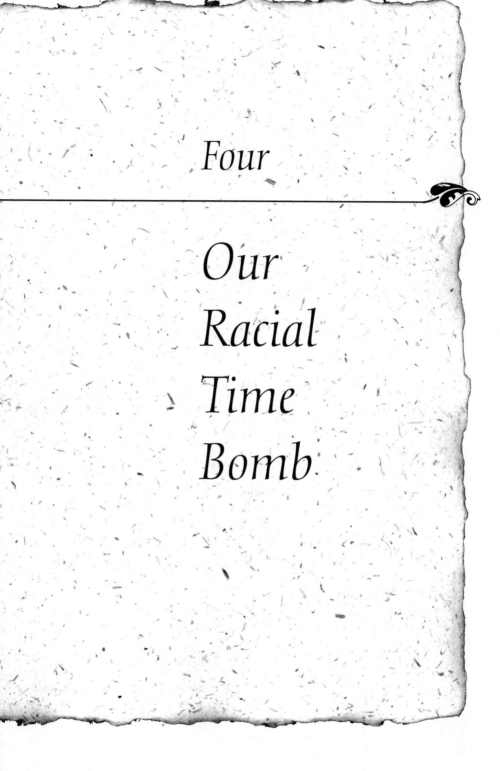

Four

Our
Racial
Time
Bomb

No aspect of our society causes me greater apprehension than the lamentable state of our race relations. I sorrowfully predict that racial tensions in our nation will erupt into violent racial strife in the near future. We have failed miserably to address these tensions, and now appear to be planning to continue the downward trend by cutting back on the already all too meager resources needed to ameliorate the conditions that have led to interracial stress.

Let me make my personal attitudes on race clear right now. I was married to a wonderful Japanese woman, born in this country of parents born and reared in Japan who had emigrated here for a better life. In forty years of married life my wife and I never encountered racial hostility, but I sometimes thought it was because I was a writer and was therefore held to different standards by others. In my books I have written at length and favorably about people of all races. I have done so because I truly believe that all men are brothers and that all races can contribute to a classless, color-blind society. Although I am critical of some of the traits and attitudes that I have recognized as being unfortunately characteristic of some of the minority groups in our society who have often led difficult lives, I do not think I can be accused of racial intolerance.

My professional life has obligated me to study intimately five of our minorities: the Hispanics, the Jews, the Native Americans, the Asians and, above all, the African Americans. The relationship between the Caucasian majority of our population and the Asian and Jewish minorities has been firmly defined; each group knows where it stands in relationship to the other, and for the most part a certain harmony prevails. Our nation's response to the growing percentages of Hispanics in our society, particularly in border areas and in other areas of high concentrations such as New York and Miami, is sometimes muddled, and we are badly confused as to what the relationship should be between our Native American minority and the Caucasian majority. Many sober students of this imbalance argue that Native Americans thrive best on the reservations that have in general been financially supported by the government. But others, like myself, believe that they do best when they are thrust into the mainstream of American life.

But the greater problem our society faces is the relationship between our African American minority and the Caucasian majority, and this problem has not begun to be solved. The longer we allow it to remain unresolved, the greater danger we face of racial violence.

Even as I drafted this chapter, additional proof surfaced of the persistence of hatred between the races in American life. The federal government announced that a total of thirty-two black Christian churches in the South had been burned. Some people who wish our black citizens ill claim that blacks themselves set the fires. There was a partial verification of this charge when police in a southern town arrested two black men accused of torching and destroying a black church. Others have argued that the acts were not antiblack but anti-Christian, proved by the fact that several of the burned churches had predominantly white congregations. Any tortured reasoning that attempts to explain away the racism simply makes this ugly epidemic more painful.

Just a sampling of statistics shows the dreadful socioeconomic imbalances between the races. Some of the data below come from reports on the 1990 Census, others of sometimes more penetrating quality from the current Bureau of the Census population surveys and the Bureau of Justice statistics. I shall intersperse these sources with data from stories in the media and studies by nonprofit research and advocacy organizations.

Income: The median income of white males in 1993 was $21,981; of black males, $14,605. In 1993 the median income of white families was $39,300; of black families, $21,542.

Affluence: According to data from the 1993 Current Population Survey of the U.S. Census Bureau, of the top 5.7 percent of all U.S. households in 1993–those with an annual income of $100,000 or more–92 percent were white and only 3.7 percent were black.

Poverty: Census data in 1993 also show that only 12.2 percent of the white population existed below the poverty level; of blacks, 33.1 percent. And 9.4 percent of white families but 31.3 percent of black families lived in poverty. The income level for poverty varies by family size; the poverty threshold of a typical family of four, for example, was $14,763 per year in 1993.

Employment: The employment data are even more divisive than the income data for the crucial group of young males between the ages of eighteen and twenty–nine; 8.1 percent of whites were unemployed in 1994, as opposed to 18.1 percent of blacks, according to the Bureau of Labor Statistics.

Babies: According to government statistics, 3.6 percent of white teenage girls between the ages of fifteen and nineteen had babies out of wedlock in 1994, but among the black girls it was 10.1 percent. Of all the births to unmarried teens in this age group a year earlier, in 1993, 17.8 percent of the whites but 31.6 percent of the blacks had had at least one previous child. Another statistic is even more disturbing for both races: in 1994, 67.6 percent of the babies born to white teenagers aged fifteen to nineteen and 95.3 percent of babies born to black teenagers in the same age range had unmarried mothers.

Criminal behavior and imprisonment: One statistic is interesting because its shocking implications have resulted in much citing of it and moralizing; I myself was guilty of circulating the statement that more black males are in U.S. prisons and jails than are in U.S. colleges. The statement is true but misleading because it includes *all* black males, even those beyond the normal age for college, according to a Bureau of Justice statistician. When the data are restricted to the age range of eighteen to twenty-four, according to that statistician,

> In 1992 there were about 149,000 black men, ages eighteen to twenty-four, in local jails, state prisons or federal prisons. That same year, there were approximately 356,000 black males, eighteen to twenty-four, enrolled in colleges in the U.S.

Nevertheless, a recent study by a nonprofit group in Washington that supports alternatives to imprisonment says that nearly one in three black men in their twenties is imprisoned or on probation or parole. According to this report, 32.2 percent of all black men aged twenty to twenty-nine are under some form of supervision by the criminal justice system. Some scholars expect this figure to rise in the next few years.

Fatalities: There is another related statistic that admits of no argument, the National Center for Health Statistics' 1992 report on mortality rates: homicide is the leading cause of death among black males aged fifteen to twenty-four.

All of these figures add up to a devastating condemnation of the conditions under which our black minority, particularly our black men, live in the United States. Decisive national action must be taken to improve the lives of our black minority, both because it is the right thing to do and because it will be necessary if we are to avoid national strife.

Now, I can hear the well-to-do white businessman saying, 'Many other groups in American history have experienced difficult circumstances and certainly no help was extended to them, but they improved their lives nevertheless. Why should blacks be treated any differently?'

I once made a study of how the Irish immigrants of the mid-nineteenth century adjusted to life in a variety of conservative New England towns. Statistics proved that the Irish initially had been treated just as harshly as the blacks. Political warfare exploded, and again and again the first Irishmen to achieve political office went to jail for theft of public funds or other abuses. Often, I judged, they had been railroaded by their Anglo-Saxon opponents.

When I asked a notable Irish politician to explain how the Irish had broken free, he laughed: 'We Irish had a trick up our sleeves. Still do. We produced a steady supply of handsome young men who could play football, and just as many beautiful girls who would grace any salon. The Irish boys went to Harvard and Yale, where they played on the teams and married their teammates' Protestant sisters. At the same time the Irish football heroes introduced *their* teammates to their beautiful Irish sisters. In time this produced a heady mix out of which grew Irish political freedom and power.' He then added a caveat that has affected my thinking: 'The tremendous advantage, however, that we Irish had over the blacks was that we were white. Our children could mix in without being visibly stigmatized. The black stands out inescapably and he cannot lose himself in the mass. I would not like to be a black. Being Irish was bad enough.'

Because of my experiences with the Irish of New England, I have often told groups of young blacks I've met with in schools

or assemblies: 'I'd love to be a teenaged black boy with intellectual gifts or athletic skills. Believe me, I would play this white society like a violin. Everybody would want to be my friend. Doors
would be opened. Colleges and universities would seek me out
and shower scholarships on me. And when I finished graduate
school in law or business or science, businesses would be fighting to employ me. I'd be much more valuable to them than the
ordinary white young man.'

I still believe this without question. America would be hungry
to get such a young black man, but then I have to admit the folly
of the fantasy. A black boy would still be black with all the im-
pediments that that involves in American life. He could not, like
the Irish boys in New England, mask his color. He might play
football for Harvard or Yale, but his white teammates still might
not take him into their homes during vacations or introduce
their sisters to him.

The uninformed attitude that blacks should simply pull themselves up by their bootstraps is clear in that oft-repeated complaint: 'Why don't those big black guys on food stamps and
unemployment handouts get themselves jobs and go to work?'
The complainer fails to realize that we are all to blame for having
structured our society in ways that make it extremely difficult for
the uneducated young black man to find a job. Much of the factory work that he used to do for a reasonable salary is now being
done down in Mexico or in Taiwan or Korea. There are, simply
but tragically, too few jobs for the young African American male
trying to make his way in the world.

White privileged society contributes to the problems of the
black community by the cruel practice of redlining, whereby
bankers refuse to lend money to businesses in black areas because the risk of theft, riots and fire is too great. Redlining is a
cruel procedure that condemns a district to destructive deteriora-

tion. In the bigger cities the hardworking Koreans move in to provide the required services while incurring the hatred of the African Americans they are serving. Ghettoization is a horrible way to organize a city, but I conclude that it has been willfully orchestrated by whites who refuse to see that the nation must take responsibility for improving the conditions in which much of our black minority lives. We cannot, as so many would like to do, wash our hands of them.

Too few realize that the results of ghettoization are destructive not only to those within the ghettos but also to those without. I live in Austin, Texas, the state capital and one of the fine smaller cities in the United States. It has a university of nearly fifty thousand students on campus, a vibrant social, political and cultural life and a surprising mix of whites, blacks, Hispanics and a huge number of students from foreign lands. (Sometimes at the university when classes change and students fill the corridors it looks like an Asian university.)

The city is divided east and west by a north–south double–deck superhighway, I-35, on which traffic is constant, noisy and smelly. West Austin contains many of the finest houses in the state, but Austin east of the highway has many characteristics of a ghetto. It's an exciting area, but residents in West Austin rarely venture eastward beyond I-35. Because I know I might want one day to write about Austin, a city I have grown to cherish, I have spent many afternoons probing the sectors: south, where the Hispanics center; northwest, where the big houses are; southwest, with moderate housing; and northeast, where the African Americans live. At the city's center are the state capitol, the university and the homes of many of the descendants of the early European settlers who played such a large role in Austin history. This geographic description is something of an oversimplification, but it does roughly represent the differences throughout the city.

Of special interest is the southern end of the city where the Hispanic families seem to concentrate. In no sense do they form a standard immigrant concentration; many of their families lived in Texas a hundred or more years before the first Caucasians arrived. They are the social elite of the city, or behave as if they were, living by their own patterns and too often refusing to send their children on to college.

I found in that section a remarkable Hispanic woman, Amelia Vargas, to help as my housekeeper after my wife died. She has proved a jewel, and we were passing our days quietly in my house in the university/residential area, ignoring the turmoil in East Austin, until the morning when she came to work in tears. Her seventeen-year-old grandnephew, a wonderful boy with a winning personality and good marks in school, had been killed by shots fired at random from a car passing through his neighborhood. Thus the social disarray in the ghetto area intrudes into even the more tranquil parts of our city.

Dallas, our sister city to the north, has its own ugly version of the confrontation between the affluent residential area–to the north in that city–and the ghetto, which lies to the south. A policeman explained it: 'A pair of unemployed black youths steal an ordinary used car, say a Ford or a Chevy. At dusk they start prowling the center of the city where businessmen work, trying to spot the wealthy fellow who drives a Mercedes or a Porsche or one of the very expensive new Italian cars. Inconspicuously they trail him to his home in north Dallas and watch as he drives his car to the detached garage well to the back of the mansion.

'As he gets out to park his car, they jump him, wrestle him for the car keys, steal his car and take off, one driver in the big car, the other following in the car stolen earlier that night. They whisk both vehicles to a secret shop that specializes in taking cars apart and shipping them illegally to South America or the

Caribbean. Two days later the Mercedes or Porsche may be on its way to Colombia or Venezuela.'

When I remarked to the policeman that this was an unbelievably clever tactic, the trailing of a big car to its destination and an easy spot at which to make the heist, he said 'Well, a Texan who's bought a big car won't give it up easily. Often the owner puts up a fight and gets shot.' He said the police were giving lectures to the owners of big cars: 'Don't drive that buggy into the middle of town. You'll be inviting them to chase after you.' So in Dallas, as in Austin, the ghetto can invade the quiet residential areas.

Not only whites but the black community, too, must work to solve its problems. Theft and vandalism where they live are rapidly destroying their neighborhoods.

I have twice been peripherally involved when a chain store with a branch located in a ghetto area decided it had to close down the branch to concentrate on areas that were more stable and better policed. In one case it was a five-and-dime store, in the other a branch store of a large grocery chain that did a huge business. In each case the local managers, one of whom I knew as a family friend, told me that profits were impossible because of the thefts by African Americans roaming through the aisles. The grocery manager said: 'They come in, rip open the tops of our boxes and have lunch right here in the store. We cannot afford to stay open.'

In each case there was public protest when the branches announced they were closing. Civic leaders shouted that the stores had to remain functioning because poor people deserved to be served as well as the rich. An ugly note was introduced in the debate when comparison shoppers proved that the grocery chain not only off-loaded its damaged goods or inferior products onto its branch store in the ghetto, but even charged higher prices for these inferior goods than it did for undamaged goods in the more favored branches. Public protest at this injustice proved to be irrelevant because, despite the anguished protests, the branches closed. The areas had been redlined not by heartless bankers attending only to their bottom line but, rather, by thieves.

I felt the two closings were both inevitable and justified, but I also followed another happier case in which city fathers with a feeling for social justice arranged for a beleaguered grocery store to remain in place, but with an enlarged group of watchful detectives paid for from public taxation. I applauded this effort, even though I can see obvious weaknesses were the plan widely copied. It shouldn't require a city to be terrorized before the community provides the services it must have to survive.

If black frustration grows and we do nothing to improve the economic prospects of blacks, there will be fearful consequences, and we already have one striking example of what these consequences might be. In Miami, the sudden influx of white Cubans in the late 1950s resulted in a flood of educated and industrious Hispanics who moved quickly into the workforce. Almost thirty years later, the forced emigration of mostly black Cubans, cynically thrust onto our shores by Castro's henchmen during the Mariel boatlift of 1980, resulted in a second deluge of far less desirable citizens. They consisted of criminal elements who created havoc in the camps to which they were assigned and who, in time, usurped most of the service-sector jobs traditionally held by African Americans: hospital orderlies, janitors, clerks in grocery stores, practical nurses. Many blacks in Miami were thus deprived of their means of earning a living. And an even more galling disadvantage faced them: to keep or find the kinds of jobs in Miami that blacks had always filled, blacks found that they must now learn Spanish. Their ancestors had been in America for hundreds of years, the Hispanics in Miami only thirty years, yet the blacks had to surrender to newcomers. Blacks went on a rampage in 1989 that tied up the city for several days and destroyed much property. Rebellion, when one group feels it has been victimized by another, is an understandable form of social protest.

I have long been a supporter of affirmative action as a means of helping disadvantaged blacks. In the 1930s I was profoundly impressed by the results of a study I made in a postgraduate class of the workings–or machinations–of an important union of electrical workers. The members, wanting to keep the union small so that they and their sons and nephews would always find a profitable job, had restricted the number of members. In the course of the century not a single African American had ever attained membership–indeed, had never even been considered for membership. Grievous damage was being done black workers by restricting equal employment opportunities.

In my study I concluded that similar historic wrongs have been inflicted on our black population in many fields, a carryover from the days of slavery and the poll–tax device of refusing blacks the vote. I became an ardent supporter of moves toward affirmative action; an evil had been perpetrated and a correction was called for.

I even supported quota systems. If a community had never had any black police officers even though a significant percentage of its population was black, this was ipso facto an imbalance that ought to be corrected. I saw nothing wrong with some agency of the government handing down an order such as this: 'The next three promotions to the police force must go to African Americans.' I became so convinced this was a justifiable move that I advocated it in all aspects of American life. Did the private schools in which I had taught have no black students? They'd better get some. Did my distinguished college have none? Rectify that immediately. Did a business tycoon who was a friend of mine have almost no black employees? Advise him to hire some right away.

Did prestigious law schools and schools of medicine admit almost no black students? Order them to alter their policies.

I was so stubborn about this aspect of our national life, and so firm in my belief that wrong *had* been done to our black population, that I failed to consider the weaknesses in affirmative action until they were pointed out by black scholars like Thomas Sowell. First, any quota system rigorously enforced runs the risk of promoting inadequately trained minority members over adequately trained whites. Second, the black student or fireman or policeman runs the risk of being scorned by his peers for having gained his position by color rather than by merit. Third, a quota system by definition casts a shadow over the entire group being favored and is therefore ultimately unfair to the African American who *is* qualified. Supreme Court decisions have forced me to restudy this inflammable subject. Also, of great importance, I failed to see the degree of bitterness that affirmative action would inspire in the working class; nor did I foresee that the anger of workmen would be directed at the Democratic Party. But despite its negatives I remain committed to the principle of affirmative action and its subsidiary, the quota system, when required to correct egregious imbalances.

Welfare is another government program designed to help blacks–and whites–living in poverty. While I am committed to the principle that the less fortunate should have a safety net, I recognize there are problems with our current system. That well-to-do businessman who rants so irrationally against the welfare system and says blacks should pull themselves up by their bootstraps like everyone else does, however, legitimately have much to complain about. I have known two black women, whom I will call Salome and Norma and who are prototypes of many stories that have circulated. Together they epitomize both the experiences of African American women and the problems of our current system of welfare assistance. Both in their early thirties, each had been married to a husband who had casually disappeared, leaving his wife with no funds or child support. Each had children, Salome a lively six, Norma a more restrained three.

There the similarities end, for Salome was a heavy-drinking, raucous party girl whose six children were sired by five different fathers, while Norma was quiet and almost demure and had suffered when her husband deserted her. Salome had a home teeming with children whom she did little to control; Norma was a frugal housewife whose two rooms with minimal conveniences nevertheless formed a real home in which she carefully reared her son and two daughters.

Although both were poor, the two young women had experienced radically different economic histories. Salome was the third generation of women in her family to exist on public welfare, and almost complacently she took for granted that her six children would pass easily onto the relief rolls when they became adults. Her oldest daughter, unmarried, was already pregnant with her second child.

Salome's family finances were minimal: a total of $313 a week for herself and her children from Aid to Families with Dependent Children; $608 per month in food stamps; and approximately $1,040 a month from the local housing authority for a four-bedroom home and her monthly electric, gas and water bills.

She achieved notoriety when a newspaper wanted to write about a family headed by generations of women without husbands. Someone directed the reporters to Salome, who proved to be a perfect subject. Brassy, outspoken, witty and wildly self-defensive, she said she was proud of her six fatherless children and had brought them up to be good citizens, except for the older boy who was already in jail–'No fault of his.' She could not, however, explain how someone else had been guilty of the armed robbery. In her justification of her lifestyle she gave a memorable quote: 'I have a right to have as many children as I want, and it's the job of the government to take care of them.'

As mentioned before, sedate Norma's husband, too, had vanished, leaving her with three children to care for and with only the most meager income from a part-time janitorial job at the local carpet factory, a job Norma inherited from her mother, who had inherited it from *her* mother. Since it was likely that Norma's daughter would inherit the job, four generations had lived in the same house. Norma's minimal salary could not have paid the rent on the old house the family had always occupied, but the safety net provided by our government for just such a family unit as Norma's swung into action to provide assistance with food stamps and money from the local housing authority and from Aid to Families with Dependent Children.

First, Norma received $160 per month from AFDC and a housing allowance from the local housing authority of about $775 a month, of which about $125 would go toward her utility bills. Like Salome, she received food stamps from the local Department of Human Services, about $320 per month for four persons. With them, she taught her three children how to purchase with extreme care. A local charity provided the respectable family with a constant flow of clothes that had been discarded by other families, and the pastor of her African Baptist Church, awed by Norma's resolute courage, saw to it that from time to time she received small gifts from church funds. Adequately nourished and housed by the welfare assistance augmenting their mother's meager income, Norma's oldest child wanted to be a policeman when he grew up, while the two girls wanted to be nurses.

Norma's was a devout Christian family, the precise kind that the safety net had been established to salvage. But when white folks saw flaming Salome and heard her challenge to society, 'I produce children, you take care of them,' they lumped the two families together and condemned them both as black women endlessly producing babies that we have to support with our tax dollars.

Our welfare system does require an overhaul–there is too much waste and too much incentive for women like Salome to remain indefinitely on the welfare rolls–but we cannot allow welfare benefits to be reduced so severely that it fails to alleviate legitimate need like Norma's. To do so will lead to even more frustration and despair in our ghettos.

Government intervention such as affirmative action or welfare assistance is not enough, however. Leaders in the black communities must also step in against destructive influences. For, although I became and remain a champion of African American rights, my enthusiasm is sorely tested when some group of black rap artists comes to town and preaches race hatred, the denigration of women and the general disruption of society. I listen in horror and I'm terrified by the nihilism espoused by such groups. Fortunately there have been outcries from both whites and blacks against such messages of hate being fed to our youth.

I was myself a partner in an interracial marriage, and it was always understood that if my wife and I had had children, we would certainly not have objected if they expressed an interest in girls or boys of another race, including blacks. But I would have been terrified by a daughter's associating seriously with a black man who subscribed to those teachings of violence or the denigration of women. I would have urged her to study the relationship carefully or perhaps find some young man, whether black or white, with more stable attitudes.

Just how serious the race problem has become in America is evident in some of the extraordinary events of 1994–95, a pivotal year in race relations: heated controversy over a scholarly treatise on race and intelligence; the O. J. Simpson murder trial; and Colin Powell's leap to fame and national acceptance as a political aspirant.

The issue of racial superiority or inferiority based on intelligence has long been with us. In 1917, during World War I, the United States instituted a nationwide draft of young men for military duty. To estimate the inherent abilities of the millions of draftees the army administered what was then called an intelligence test. It consisted mainly of verbal and mathematical questions that high school students should have been able to answer. In that massive sampling and in almost every major one that followed regardless of its purpose, blacks scored so far behind whites that serious scholars felt justified in concluding that blacks were genetically inferior to whites. Indoctrinated with that belief, I accepted it.

On my own, however, I started at about age seventeen to question this assumption. I looked at the cases of outstanding blacks of that period and concluded that some at least were certainly as able as the brightest whites I knew. I also became aware of the possible social causes for the discrepancies: poor education, deprivations that persisted even after slavery, and the fact that blacks were so restricted culturally that their children lacked the general information available to whites. I was astounded to learn how many black schools of those days did not even attempt to offer science classes.

In 1994 two reputable scholars, Richard Herrnstein and Charles Murray, published a study of race and intelligence. Their book was called *The Bell Curve*, a term lifted from statistics. The curve is a beautiful device showing the probable distribution of almost any large body of data. With the flowing outline of a bell–tall in the middle where most of the numbers will concentrate–it tails away symmetrically at each end down to a flat termination. What it illustrates is that on any testable subject, the bulk of the population will be average, with a few way below average at the flattened end to the left, a few high above average at the flattened end at the right.

When the data relating to human intelligence are compressed into a bell curve, most of us find a place in the respectable average area in the middle, but an irreducible number of us are imbeciles, at the flattened end to the left of the bell, compensated for by an equal number of geniuses at the flattened end to the right.

When Murray applied the discipline of the bell curve to military statistics, black soldiers tended to cluster in the left half of the curve, toward inadequacy, while whites clustered in the right-hand portion, indicating a modest superiority. Some of the statistics measuring the higher thought processes showed a huge difference between the able white soldiers and their less fortunate blacks.

When *The Bell Curve* hit the stands, a fiery debate ensued and there was a temptation for popular journals to say that the book proved that blacks are genetically inferior. It proved nothing of the sort, nor did it claim to have done so; it merely reinforced what we had already known back in 1917 after those first reports from the army tests: blacks do not do well in standardized tests on subject matters with which whites have a cultural edge because they learn about such subjects at home and in their superior schools.

The 1994–95 debates concerning *The Bell Curve* have sounded a warning against accepting or promulgating any easy conclusion that whites are genetically superior to blacks. Such false doctrine is dangerous to the health of our republic and should be protested vigorously. The fact that as late as the 1990s some people could still misinterpret statistics to support their beliefs in the genetic inferiority of *any* race proves how far we have to go.

It was in the same period that we saw a historic example of how deeply affected by racial tensions and hatred our nation's supposedly color–blind judicial system is. The gruesome murder in a swanky Los Angeles neighborhood of a beautiful white woman in her early thirties and her casual friend, a handsome young man in his twenties, was to deeply upset our nation and our judicial system. When it became known that the dead woman was the ex–wife of the idolized black football star O. J. Simpson and that he was the prime suspect, I muttered to myself: Oh hell! This will put race relations back fifty years.

I had first met Simpson, that superlative athlete, when I opened a long television show with him with a horrible gaffe by asking about his football career at UCLA. He was a little taken aback by my error but he said genially: 'It was USC. But don't be embarrassed. A fellow last week thought it was Stanford. At least you have the right city.' We had a lively interview, and his graciousness made me a fan.

I worked with him again in Florida when I was appointed the impartial czar of an unusual international competition, for big prize money, between the athletic stars of a dozen nations. Each contestant was eligible for ten events, but the swimming champion could not compete in the swimming races nor the tennis player in singles or doubles. The competition was furious; my friend O.J. tore the place apart in baseball, tennis and weight lifting. In the latter event foreign competitors besieged me, demanding that I rule against O.J. in a contested lift, and in retrospect I think they were right. But he had mesmerized me, and I handed down a decision in his favor that sealed the overall victory for him and helped him win a bundle.

The last time I saw him was on a blizzardy day in Shea Stadium in 1973 during a game against the New York Jets. I was a guest of the home team and, wrapped in blankets, had a superb view of the snowy field. Excitement was high, because if Buffalo's star running back, O. J. Simpson, had a good day, he would set an unbelievable record for rushing two thousand yards in a single season. Even though I sat with the Jets, I cheered for Simpson, and late in the day he made the final six yards, which put him over the two thousand mark. But on the next play a New York tackle banged through the line and threw Simpson for a loss, which put him back below the record. But he remained in the game and on a later play ripped off the necessary yardage, whereupon his coach pulled him out of the game to safeguard his record: 2,003 yards.

So I was more intensely interested in the murder case than the ordinary citizen. O.J. was my man, a true hero and a very pleasant man to work with. I hoped that he was not guilty, but as the gruesome details unfolded I was shaken by their implications. Bit by bit the cruel evidence accumulated until even I had to admit that he had probably committed the crime. But then I took refuge in a question that many people think will never be answered: How could one man kill two people and not get blood everywhere on his body? It must have been two assailants, not O.J.

The judicial system began to unravel when the sensible, soft-spoken John Macky, leader of the Los Angeles African American community, led a committee of fellow blacks into the offices of the district attorney, Gil Garcetti, and told Garcetti that he should not demand the death penalty for someone as distinguished and well loved as O.J. I was shocked when Garcetti kowtowed to their moral blackmail.

When the jury was impaneled, I wrote this note to myself: 'If the jury, consisting mostly of African Americans, votes him innocent, it will suggest that no black defendant, regardless of what he has done, can be found guilty in racially divided Los Angeles; and, if he is by some miracle found guilty, the city will once more explode in riots and burnings. If, as I feel sure will be the case, the jurors are unable to reach a unanimous verdict, so that a hung jury results, a fearful chasm will open between whites and blacks. We face a lose–lose–lose proposition.'

In the early days of the trial I felt that the lawyers on each side disciplined themselves to keep the animosities of race out of the courtroom. But slowly, seeping out like an evil miasma, race took its inescapable place in the courtroom. In poll after poll the results tended to be the same. Whites–75 percent thought the testimony condemned O.J.; blacks–75 percent believed the L.A. police had framed him. Few paid any attention to the two young people who had been murdered.

As the trial dragged to a conclusion the brilliant legal group defending Simpson achieved a miracle. They converted the trial of O. J. Simpson for a double murder into a wide–swinging attack on the L.A. Police Department, and suddenly Officer Mark Fuhrman, not Simpson, was on trial.

In the heated final moments, Johnnie Cochran, the legal eagle of the Simpson team, boldly brought race into the middle of the courtroom. In the words of his disgusted fellow lawyer Robert Shapiro: 'Not only did we play [the race card], we dealt it from the bottom of the deck.' Brazenly, Cochran begged the jurors to find Simpson not guilty as a way of sending a message to the L.A. Police Department that they must stop abusing black citizens.

When the jury retired to decide one of the most sensational legal cases in American history, they ignored the thousands of pages of testimony and the wealth of exhibits; nor did they review the arguments of the prosecution's lawyers. With breathtaking speed they took one straw vote–10–2 in favor of a 'not guilty' verdict–then the ten proceeded to persuade the two recalcitrants to vote unanimously in favor of acquittal.

On the Tuesday when the vote was announced, I, like most of America, listened with nail-biting attention as the clerk announced the–to me–appalling verdict. I may not have been 100 percent correct in my guesses on what the verdict would be, but I stand by my evaluations of the *effects* of the verdict, whatever it was to be. Race relations *were* at the crux of the case.

I was badly shaken by the vote and told my friends who had watched the proceedings on TV with me that we should keep our mouths shut because we don't want to say anything that we'll regret later. I then went to a faculty meeting, at which I made the same suggestion, and we all abided by it.

Later, watching television's incessant treatment of the verdict with learned men and women commenting on its implications, I chanced to see the disturbing shot of the students' union at Morehouse College, a black institution in Atlanta, where the students broke into paroxysms of joy when the verdict was announced. I was shattered to hear the Morehouse student union echo with boos and hisses when the cameras in the Los Angeles courthouse panned to the distraught white families of the two murdered victims.

In that awful moment I caught a glimpse of the years ahead. Blacks will make O. J. Simpson and Johnnie Cochran their national symbols of revenge. Blacks who serve on juries will be expected to bring in not–guilty verdicts whenever a brother is on trial, and worst of all, those decent middle–class whites who have slowly made themselves able to see and understand the just complaints of blacks will harden their feelings.

Although initially I thought it would put race relations back by half a century, on reflection I think the Simpson trial has probably sped the denouement of our racial tribulations forward by fifty years. With the Simpson verdict, all that I had been writing about in this essay as a problem needing attention was transformed into a crisis of great urgency. May we have the courage and wisdom to deal intelligently with this crisis so that the climax is not a violent one.

In the aftermath of the trial the Reverend Louis Farrakhan astounded me by summoning the black men of America to a huge demonstration on the Mall in Washington, and about a million African American men of all ages convened peacefully to dedicate themselves to a more responsible public and family life. They behaved impeccably; there was not a single arrest; and, they tacitly made it clear that henceforth they were a political force that white America would have to respect. There was, however, also the implication that if adjustments were not made to correct racial inequalities, there would be serious disturbances.

One interesting aspect of the Simpson case involves the eventual possibility of General Colin Powell for the presidency; until Johnnie Cochran and O.J. exploded in their faces, an encouraging number of Americans, *white* Americans, indicated they were prepared to accept an African American president or vice president. Now how will they react? Even though Powell has indicated he is not yet ready for a national campaign, will voters in the future intensify their support for him on the grounds he might prove a healing agent, or will they have serious second thoughts about raising any black into a national symbol and shy away from Powell?

That Colin Powell appears to have retired from the 1996 campaign is the nation's loss. (As of June 1996, Dole reportedly was still courting Powell for the Republican ticket.) A team of Bob Dole and Colin Powell might prove unbeatable, and Powell could run as president in 2000. If sometime in the future Powell does become president, he might go far in healing the breach between the white and the black races.

America's looming racial crisis, intensified by the Simpson trial and verdict, leads us to the crucial, inescapable question regarding race in the United States: 'Have relationships deteriorated so badly that interracial conflict has become inevitable?' I believe

the answer is Yes. All signs point to an oncoming clash, and I estimate that it will occur in the early years of the next century. I
assess the inevitability this way: First, I can see no likelihood that
white society will modify its economic practices so as to provide
employment for black males in the inner cities. They will remain
an unintegrated mass and a source of deep troubles and dislocations. Second, our national leaders not only appear unable to de-
vise a system that is not anathema to the taxpaying citizenry for
giving spending power to our lower-level citizens, but they are
also indicating that our government is actually going to back-
track on our already insufficient previous efforts. Third, current
proposals intended to diminish the number of illegitimate births,
particularly among black teenagers, are laudable insofar as taxpayers are concerned, but will be ineffective among the blacks
and whites on welfare. The proposals I've seen penalize the children, and fail to educate their bewildered parents. Fourth, im-
probable as this may sound, there may be an inherited hatred
between blacks and whites, simmering far back into the days of
slavery, and if this is true, it militates against any efforts to erad-
icate it now.

I am convinced that the ugly gap between white and black
cannot be easily bridged. I expect the animosities to intensify
into social, political and particularly economic rebellion as blacks
experience the hopelessness in the inner cities, areas that will
grow in size and in their ghetto quality. I think there will one day
be irredentist movements in which black communities will want
to govern themselves, and I suspect that vigorous protest of some
kind will erupt, as it has in so many societies in the past when attempts were made to keep an underprivileged class perpetually
downtrodden.

And now, when the political trend of our national life is already skewed against our African American citizens, various gov-

ernment agencies are beginning to reverse gains the blacks have painfully achieved in recent years. The Supreme Court, which no longer contains an African American justice philosophically disposed to defend their rights, hands down one verdict after another clearly signaling that the days of progress toward equal justice are past. Governor Pete Wilson in California focused his run for the presidency with a powerful assault on affirmative action, and the vaunted contracts of the Republican victors in the 1994 elections brought only bad news to blacks. Every cheap politician is able to gain points by shouting that talented white men in all fields are being deprived of jobs by African Americans through quota systems. It seems as if our entire society is kicking the black man and growling: 'Get back in line. Remember your place.' And all this is taking place without any serious effort to create new jobs or help the inner cities.

Recommendations

In a period of major political change when national priorities are being redefined, we must not use the need for adjustments as an opportunity to knock the blacks even further down the socio-economic ladder.

1. We must all assume responsibility for solving the most difficult problem in race relations: how to provide employment opportunities for young black men in the seventeen–thirty age bracket, particularly in the inner cities. We must not humiliate African American youth by punitive measures that attack women and children and diminish even further the chances young black men have for finding employment. For the safety of the nation our young African American men should be kept in jobs, not in jails. Employment for young men is a major factor in strengthen-

ing black family life. I sometimes fear, however, that the evils of the abandoned center city cannot be solved without a major modification of the entire economic system, which is unlikely, but I also know that some rectification is absolutely necessary. To ignore the present injustices is to invite later retaliation as world history demonstrates.

2. Wise leaders among us–economists, political leaders, social planners and dreamers of a better day–must be challenged to find solutions, and any committee directed to assume the responsibility must include ample representation of blacks and other minorities.

3. I see the need for some new type of affirmative action that avoids those parts of a quota system that have enraged many white workers who feel disadvantaged because blacks received preferential treatment. How this can be achieved with fairness I do not know, but I do know that start-up black businesses deserve help in their competition with whites'. I am also convinced that such public services as the police and fire departments must have a representative proportion of black members, and I hope this could be ensured by the pressure of public opinion rather than by numerical quotas. Common sense could be the guide. But in an impasse, or when gross abuse can be proved as in the case of the electrical union that had never admitted a single black, I would want the courts to impose a temporary quota system, which would last only until the gross imbalance was corrected. I believe the public would support such an imposition.

4. Many thousands of women on public assistance are producing illegitimate children, the new crop of babies who will likely spend a good part of their lives on relief. Somehow this constant replenishment of relief cases must be halted. Certainly when

more than 50 percent of black babies in an area are born out of wedlock, something very wrong is taking place. I cannot favor the draconian proposals for stemming this tide that are being circulated at present–they penalize the children and their mothers without solving anything–but effective programs must be developed to reestablish the black family.

I have studied the problem of illegitimate children in many different societies, and it is quite clear that they can thrive, despite moralistic attacks and the pressures of local prejudice. But I am also certain that it is better for a child to be born into and raised by an orderly family. I do not praise illegitimacy, but I salute the numerous young people who survive it remarkably well. I can speak with some authority on the subject, because I have never known what my parentage was; I was raised in a family that had no man on the premises. The three sisters who cared for me–one a nurse, one a school principal, one a loving, caring woman who bound us together–were better and stronger than many fathers in the area. Nevertheless, I am strongly in favor of the traditional American family. Statistically it is the preferable solution, and our black population would be better served if it could move in the direction of the stable family. But for this to happen, there must be jobs for the fathers.

5. We should mount a national program to encourage black families to adopt black babies. And we should halt the ridiculous propaganda from black social workers who claim that only black families can adopt black babies. Along with Oscar Hammerstein, I served on the board of Pearl Buck's Welcome House, an orphanage specializing in the placement of half-caste babies, especially black Asian, usually in the homes of white families, and we had conspicuous success. In fact, we almost never had a failure, and we had the same good luck with the all-black orphans we

placed in all-white homes. I understand the cultural basis for the rule that black babies must go only into black homes, and I can see why adult black social workers would try to enforce that rule, but I fear they do so for their own personal reasons and to the detriment of the black orphans.

6. I repeat, contentious race relations may be the most serious threat to the stability of American life. Anything we can do to achieve reconciliation must be done.

Five

Producers versus Consumers

The problem explored in this chapter was il-
lustrated in newspaper articles about three significant interre-
lated events in America's economic life. The first was headlined:
JOB CUTS AT AT&T WILL TOTAL 40,000. The second announced that
Wall Street was so excited about AT&T's move that the Dow Jones
industrial average rose sixty points. The third development appeared in the day's quotations, which showed that AT&T's common stock had also jumped upward 2⅝ and that the company
was responsible for 7.6 index points in the Dow.

The meaning of this news was easily deciphered. First, the
company had discovered that it could wind up the year with a
better bottom line on profits if it got rid of its marginally surplus
workers. Second, the stock market's exultation in the prospect of
AT&T's growing profits took precedence over all else, including
the fate of company workers and their local economies. Third,
the rise in AT&T's stock meant that American business approved
of the drastic cuts in personnel, because investors who held the
stock would probably enjoy an even greater increase in the value
of their holdings. It was, all things considered, a banner day for
American business.

But there was gloom among the forty thousand employees
who found themselves without jobs on the third day of the new
year and with dismal prospects for replacing them. Belatedly, we

are beginning to realize that such cuts are going to hit even families whose incomes range in the $70,000–$120,000 bracket. And if the husband does find a job, it will be at a salary much reduced from what the family was accustomed to. In that case, the wife, if she is not already working, must also go to work to contribute a second salary. A deplorable result is the latchkey child, who finds no one at home when he returns from school. Families in this group are severely hurting, with many unable to afford to send their children to college.

News about the downsizing of companies has become common in recent years, and its significance is always the same. Like AT&T, the overall American economy is doing fine, but its employees are not–their earnings are not even keeping up with inflation. The nation's total income is rising, but 97 percent of the increase falls into the hands of the wealthiest 20 percent of the population. Money is *not* 'trickling down.' The spectacular rise in the Dow Jones industrial average means that citizens who already possess wealth and have it wisely invested have grown richer. The stock market directly affects only a small percentage of the population, although added wealth injected anywhere in the economic system occasionally produces some carryover to the general population. But the basic truth of a rising stock market today is that the rich become richer playing games in the market while the poor remain where they were or become even poorer. The joy of the man who profited from the rise in the Dow Jones should not blind us to the grief of the man of fifty with a family to support who is suddenly without a job.

I am reminded of that universal truth voiced by Oliver Goldsmith:

> Ill fares the land, to hastening ills a prey,
> Where wealth accumulates and men decay.

Changes in American life during the past three decades seem to prove the accuracy of the poet's lament. During recent years my attempts to help friends find new jobs have accomplished little, and at the same time I see that my graduate students who are soon to enter the labor market view with apprehension their chances of finding jobs commensurate with the years they have spent preparing for them. I do not find, in American life generally, much awareness of the tragedy of unemployment. We commiserate with the homeless and weep for the young people dying of AIDS, but we do not allow the brutal facts of mid-level unemployment to sink into our conscience. Another of Goldsmith's couplets is equally applicable to the situation:

> But a bold peasantry, their country's pride,
> When once destroy'd, can never be supplied.

The economic revolution of recent times has gone far toward destroying our 'bold peasantry,' among them the factory worker who has spent years building his skills and his value to his company but who now finds he is no longer needed because his factory has fled either eastward to Asia–Taiwan, Hong Kong, Singapore, Korea–or south to Mexico. If this drift continues much longer, I can foresee only a radical redefinition of American life.

The closest historical analogy to our perilous position today is found in sixteenth-century Spain, which ruled much of the world and controlled not only the rich Iberian Peninsula but also much of central Europe, including Austria and the Netherlands. Commerce flowed freely among this group of nations; industries in one country balanced and supported those in another, and there was a rich symbiotic interrelationship. But what impresses me most about Spain in those days was that it had one of the strongest peasant cadres in the world, stalwart men and women who had mastered agriculture, wine making, leather curing, iron fabrication and the sensible harvesting of forested lands. In 1520 they excelled in all these fields and had established a high standard by which workers in other countries were judged; cordovan leather, a Toledo blade and sherry wine were known and treasured throughout the civilized world. Spain stood preeminent in the stability of its national economy, its good government under the Hapsburgs and its military genius.

In the Spanish colonies of Peru and Mexico, the conquistadores discovered silver and gold. Yearly caravels from Peru began to sail up the Pacific coastline to Panama, where mule trains hauled the precious metals across the isthmus to be loaded onto the great treasure fleets that crossed the Caribbean and Atlantic with the treasures from Peru and Mexico, depositing them at the mouth of the Guadalquivir River.

What this newfound wealth from the colonies did was to flood the economy in Spain with unearned currency. Prices for everyday goods skyrocketed and the peasants were diverted from their normal tasks. Spaniards now bought things instead of making them. The thrifty farmers no longer worked their fields. Much of the mineral wealth mined in Peru and Mexico passed quickly through Spain to finance its endeavors on foreign battlefields. The decline of Spain began with this ungoverned influx of unearned wealth, which caused the trades and industries on which Spain had depended for her greatness to fall into disuse.

France and England were fortunate that in neither their homelands nor their colonies did they discover gold. There was no sudden bonanza within their economies; the peasants continued to harvest their fields and the workmen to pursue their trades. They enjoyed a slow, orderly and controlled growth, and within a century both nations were much stronger than profligate Spain, whose flood of unearned income brought it to stagnation, if not to ruin.

Americans should study the Spanish phenomenon–falling from supremacy down to third–rate in one century–because we are making the same errors that weakened Spain. The gold and silver mines that we have discovered are the factories in Japan, Korea, Taiwan, Hong Kong, Singapore, and Mexico. They make the consumer goods our once famous factories no longer bother with. Like sixteenth–century Spain, we buy the goods we want from abroad and allow our bold peasantry to languish without jobs. We are able to purchase so much from abroad because our tax system has constantly enriched our upper classes so that they can afford the foreign goods.

Visit my street in a typical American suburb. Parked in the driveways are cars and small trucks made in Japan. In my house the sound system that plays the music I love is totally Japanese. I've tried other makes and they cannot be relied upon to function more than half a year; the Japanese electronics go on forever, and if replacement parts are ever required, they are available and easily installed. My closet is filled with all kinds of clothes made in East Asia at bargain prices; my shoes are from either Spain or Asia. My tennis shoes are from Taiwan, as are my caps, emblazoned with the names of professional U.S. sports teams. My electric lights are made abroad, as are my inexpensive bedroom clock radios. My little camera is foreign–made, as is the film I use. My neighbor has a wonderful video camera for making movies and, minutes later, showing them on a family screen. Both the camera and the screen came from Japan. I sometimes feel that anything I pick up in my home will bear, on scrutiny, the label MADE IN JAPAN. Or MADE IN TAIWAN, MADE IN KOREA.

The young lady across the street who works as a librarian occupies a neat condo in which the kitchen is an international gourmet festival. There are cans of sliced mango from Thailand, hearts of palm from Brazil and ginger–sauce dressing from

Canada. She has stocked tins of jack mackerel from Chile, water chestnuts from China and jars of marinated artichoke hearts and capers from Spain.

In heavy industry the same buy–abroad situation prevails. What used to be made in American steel factories is now made in Asia. The wood products that we used to fabricate in Oregon and Washington are now made in the woodworking factories in Asia. When I worked in Poland I was surprised to find a factory that operated overtime. When I asked what they were making, the foreman explained: 'We found a vacuum in American industry– golf carts. Everyone uses the product but nobody in the States bothers to make them anymore. We ship them by the thousands.'

Walter Cronkite and I met the workers who were building him a sailboat–in Taiwan. Wherever I went in Asia it seemed that some enterprising entrepreneur was building things for ship-ment to the States. Most curious was an entire village in China whose talented masons were carving panels in stone for the dec-oration of expensive American hotels.

This constant flight of American industry to foreign sites was very apparent to me when I lived in Alaska. In my small town, a village set among forests, the principal industry was a thriving Japanese mill in which recently felled trees were ground into a liquid pulp. Then, right into the middle of town via the small river that ran through it, came huge ships from Japan and Korea, which siphoned the pulp into their holds and ferried it back across the Pacific. There it was transformed into high–quality specialty paper, which in turn was brought back for sale in the United States.

I witnessed the same phenomenon with the ore mines in Alaska and especially with our oil reserves in the high Arctic. Everything produced from the soil was being shipped overseas to Asia, where human intelligence–which Japan and Korea and especially Singapore seemed to have in abundance–was applied to the pulp, the ores, the timber and the petroleum to make products to be sold in the United States.

One morning as I watched a huge pulp tanker bound for a paper factory in Japan pass an oil tanker headed for a refinery in Taiwan, I was struck by the economic reality: I saw that Alaska was behaving like an underdeveloped nation. We send our natural products abroad as raw materials, and the brilliant minds of Asia convert them into goods that we buy back. We make little of our own. We've become international parasites.

Proof of this change in our national direction can be seen in the proliferation of shopping malls along the margins of established towns and cities. These ornate centers are really cathedrals of consumerism, and their allure is irresistible. I see many adverse factors in the growth of malls. They disrupt traditional shopping patterns and often cause the center of the town or city to deteriorate to the loss of everyone.

The malls have a negative influence on children, who come to regard a visit to the mall as a cultural oasis and a social pleasure when in reality it dulls and deadens the youthful imagination. When I was a boy a trip into the center of Philadelphia was an exhilarating experience, for not only were the great department stores–Wanamaker's, Gimbels, Strawbridges, Lits–ranged side by side, but there was also the theater, the Keith's vaudeville house, the art museums, the churches and the parks, and the cultural riches of the university and the bookstores. In contrast, what the average mall offers is only consumerism.

Economically, the mall prospers by importing low–cost goods manufactured abroad and selling them at bargain prices, often to the detriment of local producers. There are bargains to be found in the malls, but they come at a very high overall cost to our nation. But since malls are effective distributors of goods at attractive prices, it looks as if they will not only continue at their present level but also graduate into entirely different kinds of merchandizing centers. Already some of the more notable malls are beginning to offer some cultural benefits like big bookstores, which provide comfortable chairs for the customer who is only browsing and who wants to dip into an attractive book to see if it is worth purchasing. Such stores also offer small snack bars or coffee shops. Some malls provide space for an established church to move onto the premises, and in other malls wandering minstrels and jugglers add immense charm to the business of buying things. I have seen still others that provide work space in which local artisans can ply their trade and perhaps sell their work.

But on balance I find the mall, especially in the mid-sized city, a negative influence. It is a fitting symbol of our transformation from a nation of producers into a horde of consumers. This transformation has resulted in many evil consequences.

Because we import so much unnecessarily, we have accumulated a huge foreign trade imbalance. Almost without being aware of the change, we have shifted from being a creditor nation that others used to owe for the fine products we sold them—our steel, our automobiles, our farm implements—to being the top debtor nation in the world.

Saddled with tremendous and growing debt, we are being goaded into making stupid decisions as to how we might reduce it. Just as we moved too swiftly in accumulating it, I fear we shall react foolishly in trying to reduce it. New laws being discussed whereby money now spent on child care, aid to dependent children and food for the poor would be terminated are disastrous steps in the wrong direction.

In electing to buy from abroad rather than producing the goods in our home industries, we have forced many of our own manufacturers into near bankruptcy or the abandonment of their factories.

We have allowed or even invited our home–based factories to close down mills here and open low–wage subsidiaries abroad. The history of the maquiladora factories just across the Rio Grande in Mexico is an example of the penalties we have imposed upon ourselves. Often built with American capital and utilizing manufacturing procedures invented and perfected in the States, these Mexican factories, able to hire Mexican workers at $1.46 an hour, can undersell and bankrupt American plants that have to pay American workers $10 and more an hour. The final product created by this semislave labor is then welcomed back, tax–free, into the American markets. These factories are of great benefit to Mexico's economy, but they are nevertheless an example of industrial suicide sponsored by our own government.

These radical changes have gone far toward destroying the vitality of the American labor movement and removed from effective public life a segment of society that, despite its faults, did goad our leaders into making sensible rules regarding the working class. Absent the countervailing force of the unions, our country has made horrendously wrong decisions concerning the relations between capital and labor; the twelve years of 'Reaganomics' under Presidents Reagan and Bush were disastrous for labor. The loss of labor's powerful restrictive voice has weakened the nation.

A major penalty we incur when we shift from producer nation to consumer is spiritual, and here I must apologize for inserting into this discussion an intensely emotional credo to which I have always subscribed.

I believe a positive good results when a man assumes the obligation of a regular job; he spends at least five days a week at his tasks and has the fulfilling pleasure of knowing that he is making a product of use to his society, his town and his family. I believe this has been true since the beginning of civilization. I cannot presume to speak for women, but I do not doubt that they have the same sense of satisfaction in a job well done.

What is there in daily work that creates such a sense of well-being? I suppose it stems from memory reaching far back to a time when work meant survival, and when the avoidance of work brought disaster to oneself or to family or community. The same spiritual reward for a job well done motivated the early settlers in America, who had to clear fields for growing crops and to build log cabins for their families. By extension, I think that more recently the same motivations and satisfactions operated among the workers in the steel mills of Pittsburgh, the auto plants in Detroit or in the building of irrigation ditches in Colorado and Wyoming.

I believe it to be an obligation of the state to organize society so that the maximum number of citizens can have wage-producing work that enables them to support their families and maintain their self-esteem. The failure of the leaders who organize and manage our economy to assure such work leads to a nation on the decline; if this prolonged failure to provide jobs persists, radical changes will sweep the land. I suspect that if a wife watches her husband fail week after week to find work, or if she herself cannot find a job, before long she might well become more revolutionary than he, for she will see a monstrous wrong in the failure of society to protect her children, and she will set out to correct it and urge her husband to do the same.

I would be less than honest if I did not admit that our citizens *do* obtain certain benefits in this shift from producing to consuming. They can buy with confidence men's clothing made inexpensively overseas and for sale here at low cost as well as the foreign-made electronic products that work and are reasonably priced. The foods we import because our farmers are no longer producing them at home are delicious and worth what we pay for them. The rich variety of choice, the reliability of the items made abroad and the relatively low prices are all considerable assets, and I would not easily surrender them. But I see with painful clarity that prolonged reliance upon the workers in foreign lands–the steel fabricators, the shoemakers, the tailors–is corrupting the American spirit. We pay a fearful penalty for the bargains we enjoy.

Even so, I could approve our continuing to import many of the goods that enhance our life if we were allowed to sell our products abroad in an even, well–regulated exchange because that would mean jobs for our workers producing those goods. But it is a difficult situation because some foreign nations restrict the import of our products.

As usual, when our nation makes a radical shift in our economy the heaviest burden falls on those least qualified to adjust to the new order. The radical shifts in our economic policies have had particularly adverse consequences for three categories of the very poor: the African Americans, the Hispanics and the so-called poor whites. Figures provided by the Bureau of Labor Statistics reveal that 6.1 percent of the labor force–men and women sixteen years and older who were trying to find work–were unemployed in 1994, but blacks in this group had more than twice the percentage of unemployment (11.5 percent) as whites (5.3 percent), with Hispanics (9.9 percent) also showing a heavy disproportion.

A closer look shows the burden on certain age groups is especially onerous. Teenagers aged sixteen and seventeen are hit hardest: 19.9 percent of those trying to find work cannot. For African American teenagers in this age group the percentage climbs: 39.3 percent of the males and 32.9 percent of the girls are unemployed. Hispanic teens don't fare much better: 33.3 percent of the Hispanic male labor force and 29.7 percent of the Hispanic girls are unemployed. White male teens show an 18.5 percent rate of unemployment and white girls, 16.6 percent.

If unemployment continues indefinitely, the young people affected become especially susceptible to depression, lose their zeal in pursuing their goals and, becoming likely recruits for gang membership, later resort to overt criminality.

It would be misleading, however, to focus only on the plight of young people. Older unemployed workers, who are also affected adversely, include 6.6 percent of the labor force aged twenty-five to twenty-nine, 4.9 percent of those aged thirty-five to thirty-nine and 4.1 percent of those aged fifty to fifty-four.

In June 1995 there were 1.6 million people 'marginally attached' to the labor force who wanted work and were available for it. Of those people, the Labor Bureau says, 364,000 were 'discouraged workers' who had stopped looking for a job because they believed there was none available.

The American corporations, by moving their jobs to low-wage workers in other countries and by downsizing and cutting payroll, commit a double economic crime: they increase the ranks of the unemployed, and they drastically curtail the buying power of the very consumer groups they must rely upon to buy the goods they produce. This is insane, counterproductive behavior.

Recommendations

I see little chance that we will be willing to alter our buying habits. This means that our adverse trade balance will not only continue but also grow and that unemployment will remain an onerous burden.

1. Steps must be taken to protect our workforce, which is being discriminated against by the flight of industry to foreign lands. Either the flight must be outlawed, or the loss of salary must be compensated for by some kind of cash payment from the government or by job training both for jobs that now exist and for new forms of employment anticipated for the future. My strong preference is for job training rather than financial compensation.

2. Our planners, especially in the military, should conduct studies to determine which of our factories make products that are essential to our national survival. They should be encouraged not only to continue operating but also to improve the skills of their workers.

3. Our nation must stop stumbling backward lest we end up as a third-world power; we must reduce our exports of basic materials to East Asia, where innovative intelligence converts them into consumer goods that are shipped back across the Pacific to be sold in our stores. American brainpower should be applied to American raw materials for manufacture of American goods.

4. Distasteful as it might be to our current leaders, we would be better off as a nation if strong and capable labor unions were revived and invited to share in the making of decisions vital to our welfare.

5. I am hesitant about suggesting this final idea, because it relates to work and on that subject I am a fanatic. The spiritual value of work must be extolled. From the age of ten, when I gathered laundry from neighbors for my mother to wash, I have never, during the subsequent eighty-odd years, been unemployed. For most of my life I have worked an excessive seven days a week–with a less strenuous self-imposed regime I might well have accomplished more. Nevertheless, I have found great

joy in work and advocate it for everyone. The American tradition of the work ethic has remained strong, and most Americans still feel satisfaction in a job well done. Our government should launch drives to reestablish the workers' pride in and loyalty to their jobs. But perhaps what is most important in this era of the preeminence of the bottom line is the need for employers to be loyal to their workers.

Six

Our Educational System Must Be Revived

*A*s I prepared to write this chapter I received an unexpected letter from a former student, which provided a portrait of me as a teacher:

> It happened sixty years ago but I remember it as if it were yesterday, for it was an important day in my life. You were teaching us Shakespeare and taking it seriously when Walter Matthis began acting up with two girls in the back of the room. You paid no attention to him for some minutes, then you got real mad and said in a low voice: 'Matthis, there is no place for you in this classroom. Get out!' We were all real scared, but Walter stood up and started down the aisle leading to the classroom door. But this meant he would have to pass your desk, and you said in an even tougher voice: 'Matthis, if you keep coming this way, I'm going to punch you right in the face and lay you out flat!' He took one look at you standing there, turned around and in one movement jumped through an open window. Lucky our class was on the ground floor. After that you had no trouble maintaining discipline.

John Price, the writer of this letter, is remarkably accurate regarding that day in my life as an educator. I loved the profession and throughout my career taught in almost every grade level from kindergarten through the postdoctorate level at Harvard. Always, I took my work seriously and expected my students to do the same.

Although George School, where I was teaching, was a Quaker institution preaching nonviolence, and although my unusual behavior must have embarrassed the administration, the principal and the school board supported me without even issuing a reprimand. I had behaved in an unorthodox manner, but it was clear that I was justified in doing so. Second, Walter Matthis's parents firmly supported me by saying: 'Walter deserved it.' And, third, of great importance, the student body let it be known that they sided with me and not with Walter.

How different the schools are today. Note that in my contretemps with Walter Matthis I was teaching Shakespeare rather than remedial English but, more important, in 1935, when this incident took place, teachers had strong support from their students' families–families with high moral and social values. With their shared goal–the education of children–teachers and parents could and did work together effectively. The fact that Walter might have been embarrassed by the incident–'traumatized' in the parlance of today–was not allowed to overshadow the importance of the lesson he learned. He even became one of my good friends and a responsible student. Today if I were to be so bold as to reprimand a student like Walter in a public school, or even in a private one, his parents would raise a storm of protest and demand I be fired for my actions. If the administration defended me, which today would rarely happen, the Matthis clan might even go to court and take legal action against me or the school.

Because of the years I have spent at the variety of institutions where I have both taught and studied, I have a keen appreciation of the educational process in America and how it has changed in recent years. The nation has a strong tradition of education upon which to draw. As early as the 1640s the Massachusetts Bay Colony was passing laws requiring the townships to build schools and to teach reading, writing and arithmetic. Of equal importance, the colony also established the tradition of taxing the public to support the schools.

Surprisingly, even though Washington and Jefferson were among many of the founding fathers who stressed the need for general education in a democratic society, our Constitution does not mention education. In 1779 Jefferson was unsuccessful in his attempt to establish public education in Virginia, but by the 1850s the principle of local schools for the education of all children at public expense was widely accepted, at least in the northern states. In the states west of the Alleghenies our nation developed the remarkable system of national land grants for public schools. In Texas, before the fall of the Alamo and the final victory at San Jacinto, the Texas Declaration of Independence declared that 'unless a people are educated and enlightened it is idle to expect the continuance of civil liberty or the capacity for self-government.'

But the person primarily responsible for the creation of a nationwide system of free public education was Horace Mann, a remarkable lawyer from Massachusetts. He was, successively, a skilled lawyer, a member of the state legislature, secretary of the state board of education, a member of the national Congress and president of Antioch College in Ohio. In his spare time he toured the nation preaching his passionate belief in free public schools, so that by the 1850s the nation as a whole had come to share his views. He was indeed the father of the American public school, which he saw as the basis of a free democracy.

America's free public schools provided the ladder that enabled me to climb out of my obscure village into active participation in a great democracy. Today, in my sixty-sixth year of teaching, again in a fine university, I am increasingly mindful of H. G. Wells's warning that 'Human history becomes more and more a race between education and catastrophe.' I am more involved in education than I ever was and consider myself qualified to make the following evaluations of our schools and colleges.

First, the brightest and hardest-working students, who are the ones I see today, are better than I was at their age in the 1912–1931 period. They know more, have a wider frame of reference, do better in tests and behave admirably. The top students are an impressive lot, of whom our nation can be proud. The future welfare of our nation is in safe hands insofar as having a supply of truly bright people to help run it.

Second, the many students at the bottom of the academic pile are no worse today than those I knew in school, except that they may be limiting their opportunities further by drugs. I regret to say that they seem largely incapable of absorbing any education at all. Unfortunately the types of service jobs traditionally open to them—manual labor, menial tasks—are not increasing and the wage scales in the service sector are dropping to levels inadequate for economic survival. These unfortunates are a national problem that must be dealt with.

If America consisted only of the very bright at the top and the least intelligent at the bottom, our nation could exist much as Mexico has existed, with its very rich allowing just enough of the nation's wealth to trickle down to the least fortunate to forestall revolution. Fortunately for us, our nation has been able to create and nurture a large middle class on which our strength has depended. In my childhood days, my village of four thousand consisted of perhaps four hundred members of the elite at the top, six hundred disadvantaged at the bottom and three thousand of the finest middle-class people the nation has ever had—the store-

keepers, the secretaries, the people who worked as farmers cultivating the land, the schoolteachers, the lawyers, the salesmen and
the large contingent who traveled each morning by train into
Philadelphia to fill mid-level jobs there.

At the age of fourteen, primarily because of my athletic ability
but augmented by my scholastic record, I leapfrogged from the
bottom group right into the center of the middle group, which
turned out to be decent and congenial. In those years, we students in the middle group were supposed to prepare ourselves
for employment in the businesses of the community. Girls
learned typing, boys were expected to master the rudiments of
learning, including a proficiency in mathematics; all were expected to learn good manners. In 1925 in my high school graduation class of about seventy, only three or four went on to
college; almost all the others were sufficiently well trained to find
employment.

How different is the fate of the middle group of students today.
Their level of education and mastery of skills are so deplorably
low that they constitute a national crisis.

The nation has a vital concern in the failure of the public
school system to provide a constant supply of young people adequately trained in language, mathematics, history and the social
sciences. Industries large and small are experiencing an inadequately educated supply of workers. I am worried about the future of our nation. A complex democracy cannot be operated by
a citizenry increasingly unable to compete in the world market-
place against the people of better-educated nations.

If our military capacities were in as much peril as are our intellectual capabilities, the nation would be taking gigantic and
immediate steps to repair the deficiencies. It is scandalous that
we are not taking equally huge steps to reverse the decline in our
basic educational adequacy.

I am frightened by this descent toward incompetence within the middle group, a decline that stems primarily, I believe, from the many unfavorable social changes I detect in the nation. When the average child of school age is allowed to spend seven or eight hours a day watching television, there is no time left for reading. Children who do not read the important books when young fail to learn the great lessons of history, and will become illiterates wedded to television.

I should say here that I recognize the positive aspects of television and what it can contribute to an education. High school students today have a much larger base of general knowledge than I had at their age. Via the electronic marvel of television they have viewed foreign countries and traveled to deserts and ice caps; they have seen what a symphony orchestra is and heard what it sounds like; those so inclined have seen and heard grand opera; they have seen the outstanding sports figures, and they have watched more high-level entertainment of all kinds than I was able to enjoy in my pre-electronic youth. I recognize the possibility that we may be in the process of developing a new kind of person, a pragmatist who ignores books and reading but who nevertheless acquires real learning through the television screen. I think it quite possible that some of our political leaders or generals or the controllers of big businesses may arise from these television-educated youth. Television may not teach one how to think, but it surely teaches one how to manipulate.

This possibility of a new type of human being does not frighten me; I am not locked into a belief that everyone of promise should attend college. The television graduate and the college graduate can exist side by side.

But I do want to make clear the practical importance of learning that comes from books and schooling. No big city, for example, can survive unless someone there has an understanding of

the engineering required for sewage disposal. Without this ex-
pertise the city would be ravaged by one deadly plague after another. Large cities also require highly trained people such as air
traffic controllers. Also essential are doctors, who know how to
treat ailing human beings, and other professionals trained to deal
with one important function or another. My point is obviously
that no community can exist without the guidance and assistance of a cadre of bright, educated people.

I am not an elitist; I do not believe for one moment that our
nation can be run only by those David Halberstam described as
'the best and the brightest.' I faced the problem of elitism when I
taught, and although I found pleasure in goading very bright
students on to higher levels of performance–better term papers,
more concentration on difficult topics–I never believed that educating the brightest was the major aim of education. The real task
of the teacher is to aid in the development of a well-rounded,
moral society in which all levels of young people can make positive contributions.

Perhaps I should clarify one thing: where others are concerned
I do not take the elitist view, but in terms of myself alone, I am
an elitist of the highest order. I want to be better; I want to confront the bigger problems; I want to make a meaningful contribution. Anyone who has similar aspirations requires the very
best education she or he can acquire. I feel strongly that we need
people who can read and write and are not couch potatoes.

Through the years I have witnessed and experienced several
trends that have made this goal more difficult to achieve. I spent
many happy years as a textbook editor at one of the premier
New York publishing companies, Macmillan, where I helped produce textbooks in a variety of subjects for use in schools across
the nation. While I was at Macmillan a radical new discipline
began to dominate the writing of schoolbooks. A highly regarded

educator and psychologist, Edward Lee Thorndike, compiled a list of words and the frequencies with which they occurred in everyday American life: newspapers, popular books, advertisements, etc. From these basic data he published a list, sharply restricted, which he said ought to determine whether a specific word should be used in writing for children. If, for example, the word *take* received his approval, use it in the schoolbooks. If *discredit* did not appear on his list, don't use it, for to do so would make the books too difficult for children.

We editors worked under the tyranny of that list, and we even boasted in the promotional literature for our textbooks that they conformed to the Thorndike List. In my opinion, however, this was the beginning of the continuing process known as 'dumbing down the curriculum.' Before Thorndike, I had helped publish a series of successful textbooks in which I had used a very wide vocabulary, but when I was restricted by Thorndike, what I had once helped write as a book suitable for students in the sixth grade gradually became a book intended for grades seven through eight. Texts originally for the middle grades began to be certified as being appropriate for high school students, and what used to be a high school text appeared as a college text. The entire educational process was watered down, level by level.

Coincident with the dumbing down of the classroom materials came a wild inflation of grades. What in my early days as a professor was judged to be a C paper was elevated to a B, and students' estimation of their own merit became so inflated that professors were berated if they did not give even the most casual student at least a B. Former B students, as judged on a realistic scale, now demanded A's. The softening of American education was under way with pernicious results.

It is well documented that discipline in today's public schools has fallen to lows that are not only regrettable but even preposterous; the average big city is unable to keep intruders with guns out of its schools. In one year at an average–sized Florida county school, more children aged fourteen to nineteen were murdered by handguns brought into their schools than adults were killed in the entire nation of Denmark. One beginning teacher told me she was warned during her training class: 'You must always make sure you have direct access to the classroom door, so you can escape if they start to come after you.' I cannot conceive how meaningful education can take place if teachers and students have to worry about protecting themselves from gunfire.

I have begun to appreciate the determination of parents so concerned about their children's education that they move them out of the poorly controlled public schools and place them, at considerable cost to themselves, in private or parochial schools. I regret this weakening of the public school, especially if decreased enrollment erodes support for the taxes that go to schools, but until the public schools are improved it is understandable that parents will make the alternate choice.

Strange as it may seem, coming from a fanatical defender of public school education like myself, I am beginning to believe that refractory students who refuse to accept classroom discipline should be allowed or even encouraged to drop out of school, perhaps as early as age fourteen and certainly at sixteen. Successful education for the majority of students can proceed if boys and girls determined to disrupt orderly procedures are kept out of class. Such committed troublemakers would not be allowed in a workplace or in any military unit; why allow them to disrupt the schoolroom? Especially when our law courts have succeeded in eroding the right of schools to discipline even the most egregious offenders.

I am aware that private schools are able to achieve favorable results partly because they are permitted to reject or expel students who pose disciplinary problems; the rejected student then goes back to the public school, which by law must accept him. I also understand why parents would pressure the government to help them pay the tuition charged by private and parochial schools, which provide much better education than the public schools. As a teacher in both private and public schools I cannot blind myself to the fact that any public school that has allowed itself to become a wasteland cannot provide the education our nation requires of its young people if we are to survive in world competition.

Allowing incorrigibles who are sixteen or even fourteen years old to drop out of school should be counterbalanced by instituting special schools organized to handle such young people. A feature of these schools would be practical training in the industrial arts. No attempt would be made to teach literature or philosophy. In addition to vocational training, simplified courses in the basic moral structure of society would be stressed: the sanctity of an agreed-upon obligation; care for the poor; the healthy rearing of children; avoidance of misbehaviors that might result in jail sentences; and the foundations of patriotism. The students must also be told that the years following graduation from high school are much tougher today than in the past. When I graduated in the 1920s, almost any boy with a sound body could find refuge by enlisting in the army, but that is no longer the case. The difference is that the computer has radically altered the army and the other services. The new technology is so prevalent and so demanding that dullards are not welcomed by the services. It is more important than ever that boys and girls learn some skills that will assist them in finding work.

I would expect that there would be a residue of incorrigibles for whom even such carefully structured schools would be incapable of accomplishing much, and we would simply have to watch with aching sadness as these students sink lower and lower. But this has happened in all societies in all times, and there seems to be little we can do for such hopeless cases. A tremendous amount of constructive results can be achieved however, with the upper echelon of difficult young people *if* their schools train them not for college but for taking their place in the national workforce.

Another important factor in the decline of our schools is the breakdown of so many American families. It has meant that the schools can no longer rely upon parental assistance, either scholarly or disciplinary. When I was a young instructor during the Depression and working with a sterling group of teachers, we conducted a running seminar on the question 'What are the essential components in the education of a child?' We spent long hours discussing our experiences with growing children and analyzed a score of factors. In the end we arrived at a list something like this:

1. *Living in a family that has an orderly dinner every night at which there is lively discussion of important subjects.*

It helps if there is a dictionary and an atlas available so that the parents can frequently say: 'Let's look that up in the dictionary,' or 'Let's see exactly where Morocco is.'

2. *Instruction in fundamental moral values.*

This can come from discussion in the home or in attendance at Sunday school or church, or–perhaps most important–by parents' setting an example by their own moral behavior. But it had better come from somewhere, and forcefully, or the child and, later, the adult, may find himself or herself adrift. These values should also be reinforced in the school.

3. *It helps if the growing child has other children to play with, and if there are no siblings, preschool is a strong substitute.*

But since this is an expensive luxury for most families, it introduces an early wedge between the affluent and the impoverished that our Head Start programs have only partially removed. Preschool is a splendid experience for children, and the Head Start programs should be expanded and improved rather than cut back as was being contemplated by the U.S. Congress in 1996.

4. *Although the first six years of schooling are very important, they do not carry the intellectual weight or significance that the later years do.*

By the seventh grade, however, rigorous intellectual instruction should take place to include basic mathematics and the ability to write in thoughtful sentences.

5. *When young students enter high school it becomes essential that they really get down to work: research in the library, mastery of plane geometry and trigonometry, familiarity with some of the great books of the world, a solid sense of world geography and, of great importance, a study of the traditions and documents of American history.*

In our little school in 1934–37 we idealists were providing our high school students with the equivalent of what colleges and even universities would be offering twenty years later. Our students responded to our sometimes harsh demands; they received an education, and most of them became first–class citizens. Those who went on to college–a majority–tended to do superior work.

Reviewing these notes sixty years later, I would not revise the scale of values. Education at the family dinner table remains in first place for me, and the seventh grade is still a great dividing line between easy educational tasks and real intellectual work.

I can imagine how frustrated I would feel in a public school today in which homework is not required and in which a shocking number of my students come from homes in which family discussions do not take place or cannot take place because there *is* no family. A great sadness overtakes me when I think of the young people who start life in such deprivation and I wonder if they can ever recover from this first crucial void.

I can speak of these matters with some authority because I grew up in an untraditional family with no man in the home. We certainly could not afford a preschool program, but we did have a free public library at our disposal and learned from the readings our mother shared with us each evening. We took advantage of every free opportunity provided by our society: picnics in a parkland, church festivals, games on the athletic field, music played on the bandstand and, above all, that constant flow of library books into the home. Reflecting on those difficult days, I can see that we had a wealth of educational opportunities, as proved by several of my fellow orphans who went on to earn high marks in college.

A final important factor in reversing the decline in the education of America's middle students is perhaps the most powerful of all–the computer. It has burst upon our society with consequences so explosive that we do not yet appreciate how much this new technology changes everything.

One expert I spoke to said he believed that in history ordinary citizens had faced two crucial moments in their painful struggle to achieve meaningful lives: 'The first came with Gutenberg's invention of a process whereby movable hand-carved type could be used to publish books. The ability to mass-produce books set men's minds free to explore all branches of knowledge. Imagine the plight of the village boy half a century earlier who might have aspired to learning. Impossible, unless he joined a monastery and became a scribe. After Gutenberg the village boy, even though he could not afford to own a book of his own, for prices were prohibitive, could with persistence and a touch of guile gain access to the five or six books in the local church or in the squire's library. The period from 1440 to 1500 must have seen bright young men proliferating across Europe, bursting with newfound energy and aspiring to new forms of employment.

'Believe me,' the expert said forcefully, 'the arrival of the computer in the past thirty to forty years is an accomplishment even *more* crucial than Gutenberg's book. In externals the two might seem basically the same–technological advances that had revolutionary consequences. But the computer carries an added dimension that makes it much more powerful and dangerous than the printed book.'

I interrupted: 'I think you're downgrading the book. Its consequences were world–shattering; because of it anyone could be a scholar. What had been arcane now became available. I doubt that from our vantage point we can appreciate the intellectual revolution produced by the availability of the book.'

He replied: 'I revere the book, but the computer is greater by several magnitudes because it deals not only with words but with all the symbols of human life: mathematics, the equations of chemistry, the catalog of genes, economic patterns, mechanical intelligence, business predictions, speculations about the beginning of the universe and the age of our world, predictions as to how much longer our world can exist before our sun explodes and engulfs us in a fiery ball of exploding hydrogen. The computer is infinite and it invites us and enables us to think in infinite patterns.

'Believe me, the chasm that already exists separating those people with computer competence from those without will widen until it becomes unbridgeable. I see no hope for the computer illiterates to acquire meaningful jobs or to secure places on the economic ladder. The computer alters everything.'

Other experts agreed with his Gutenberg/computer analogy. One said: 'Granted that when Gutenberg offered his movable type around 1455, the resulting book changed perhaps one hundred of the then most important intellectual fields, an amazing contribution. But today the computer will modify, for the better, five thousand of our pressing problems. You've got to think of the computer as an agent magnitudes more powerful than the book.'

A woman computer professor pointed out another problem that I had not identified. 'Since in the ownership of advanced computers men account for eighty percent and women twenty percent–or maybe the imbalance is as wide as ninety percent to ten percent–we women will be at a severe disadvantage in the competition for jobs in which computer competence is required. The glass ceiling is bound to be lowered every year.'

I became aware of how all-embracing the computer problem is the other day when I received a bulletin from Harvard University that listed some hundred jobs that were open at Harvard. Among a wide variety of specialties, they ranged from a position as head of a department to beginning instructors in small classes to students who reshelve books in the library. And every announcement carried the proviso: 'Must be computer-literate.'

I asked a Harvard faculty member why a young man assigned to reshelving books in the library stacks required this literacy and the professor replied: 'We work on Napoleon's principle: "Every one of my soldiers carries a marshal's baton in his knapsack." We expect the boy shelving books today to be in charge of our Greek bibliographies six years down the line.'

The gap between the young person who is able to handle computers and the unfortunate who cannot will grow ever wider, and always to the terrible detriment of the latter. Therefore, it is imperative that all schoolchildren be taught how to use the computer and word processor, for to fail to learn this technology is to condemn oneself to life as a secondary wage earner.

I must confess, however, that since I never learned the touch system of typing QWERTY–the name for touch-typing that comes from the first six keys on the standard typewriter–I myself cannot use even the word processing programs of my computer. I've slowly and laboriously typed my millions of words with two fingers on manual typewriters, but I am not completely stupid. As soon as I finish with my inept typing I turn the pages over to my gifted secretary, who puts them on her word processor, on which we do our editing. Without her help I could not function.

Recommendations

1. Since education is the lifeblood of our nation, we must do everything practical to strengthen our public schools. Of vital importance is the provision of ample funding by taxation to enable these schools to do their jobs, and to do them well. This has been a basic principle of American life for nearly one hundred fifty years. Bringing our educational system back to a level even of adequacy will not be cheap, but we must be brought to the realization that, in the words of a British academic: 'Education costs money, but then so does ignorance.'

2. High and challenging academic standards must be demanded of the students in our schools.

3. Encouragement should be given to alternate systems of education, such as the private and parochial schools, but we must guard against diverting too much money from the public sector to the private.

4. Strict discipline must be enforced. Guns, drugs, cigarettes and alcohol must be kept out of our schools. (How horrible it is even to have to include such a warning!)

5. School-leaving age should be lowered to fourteen years for children who have proved themselves too unruly for the classroom's necessary discipline.

6. Schools providing a nonacademic education—vocational training in the practical arts—should be encouraged in every community.

7. Moral stability should be a major aim of the school, which can be achieved without emphasis on any particular religion.

8. Education must include the great traditions of American democracy and the history of our nation. As early as the seventeenth century John Locke postulated the reality that 'the only fence against the world is a thorough knowledge of it,' and we must educate with this reality ever in mind.

9. All schoolchildren should have training in the use of the computer and the word processor.

10. The teaching of creationism to the exclusion of science should not be allowed.

Seven

The Family Under Fire

*I*n one of the planks in their platform for changing the character of America, the young Republicans in Congress and their colleagues on the religious right are spectacularly correct: the American family *is* in disarray and crying for help.

I am a devoted supporter of a constructive family life. In research for my books I have had to analyze the behavior of families dating back thousands of years and have been especially a student of family patterns in the United States. In the prehistoric period, insofar as we can reconstruct it, the family unit of a male, a female and their children had been established very early and was even then seen as the practical solution to the problem of how the race was to safeguard its future and ensure that infants would become responsible adults.

I am sure that some human aboriginals must have wondered why it was that so often in the animal kingdom a newborn infant could begin to function ably almost at birth, while the human child required about one and a half years to become minimally self-sufficient. Nothing can be more remarkable than the baby giraffe with its spindly legs able to walk erect the first day, or more mind-boggling than the newborn kangaroo, no bigger than a mite, who without assistance can make its way around its mother's body to the comforting pouch in front in which it matures. But the human young requires years of patient nurturing by both mother and father. The concept of the human family, for the purpose of providing care for children, has remained vital in our society.

I must assume that through the millennia the prototypical family existed and flourished in response to some deep human need. If it has persisted for so long, its worth has been fully tested, and I think it deserves our unqualified support today.

This chapter focuses on the American family as a worthy social agency in deep trouble, and on what political changes should be initiated to give it assistance. First, I discuss, as background, the characteristics of the American family starting in the early 1600s in New England and Virginia and continuing into the first half of this century. Second, the focus is on the assaults that have been made on the traditional family since World War II, particularly through changing sexual mores, alterations that have occurred in the traditional forms of courtship and marriage, the growth of nontraditional families, and the difficult problems experienced by older married couples. Third is the difficult question of what political steps should be taken to provide the family with additional support. I shall also digress upon a particular interest of mine: How can young women of superior training, character and skills find young men to marry? (The surprising success of recent motion pictures like *Little Women* and those based on the Jane Austen novels that deal with husband hunting prove that the subject is still of importance to young people today.)

The early American family. In both New England, as in the Plymouth Colony, and in Virginia at Jamestown, the frontier family was almost rigidly defined, with each member assigned tasks that he or she had to perform without complaint. The father cleared his property of trees, a job requiring long hours and backbreaking toil.

He was also expected to build the log cabin to house his family. And when this was done, he had to till the soil and plant his crops. He commonly died in his late forties, an old, worn-out man.

The colonial wife worked equally diligently. Her tasks required less heavy physical labor but were just as exhausting as those performed by her husband: spinning wool into thread, endless sewing and patching by hand, churning milk to make butter, tending to household chores, planting and cultivating a garden, often assisting her husband to sow his fields with grain and harvest it when it ripened and, of course, raising the family's children. She too died young in her early forties after bearing six or seven children, at least several of whom died in infancy.

The young boy and girl also had well-defined tasks; they helped their parents by doing various chores, such as chopping wood for the fireplace, learning to spin and sew if you were a girl, helping with the garden and, most demanding of all, mastering the school lessons on which their futures depended. At night, by the light of the fireside, they read either their next day's lessons or one of the precious books obtained by their parents.

As the children reached age sixteen or seventeen, they became attracted to the young neighbors of the opposite sex, and by eighteen or nineteen the young people would marry and start families of their own. I have never seen a reliable study of how the young men and women who did not find partners in those early years of courtship existed in a frontier society. Their lot could not have been enviable, but in the early literature of our nation we do find examples of the unmarried aunt who remained with her sister or brother when either of them married, so perhaps that was the norm. But a good deal of active family planning and devising occurred in the effort to find a husband for the unmarried daughter or niece. I have a less clear picture of how the unmarried man survived.

So in the colonial family everyone knew his or her place and what was expected, and deviation was neither allowed nor forgiven. Inevitably there was deviation, as Nathaniel Hawthorne showed with such compassion in his novel *The Scarlet Letter,* in which Hester Prynne was caught in adultery and paid a terrible price for it. And there was always the risk for an older woman living alone that she would be accused of being a witch and condemned to be submerged in water after being strapped into the ducking stool or even be hanged.

In the course of my research on the settlement of Colorado I read scores of journals of the families who in the 1840s made the covered-wagon trek from New England or Pennsylvania clear across the continent to California or Oregon. The travail that this involved is staggering for the modern reader to imagine: broken wheels, dead oxen, cholera sweeping the entire trail like a plague, being snowbound in blizzards, diminishing food supplies and death en route. It was a wonder anyone made it to his or her destination, but most did.

Motion pictures and television, not satisfied with the dangers listed above, have added the inevitable attack by Indians in which the trekkers bravely fight off the savages. Pure bunk! The record is that almost never did the Indians attack a wagon train; they watched from afar. If the would-be settlers fired at them because they felt threatened, the Indians did retaliate, but never in large numbers or with much effectiveness.

Out in the West the general characteristics established by the colonial family persisted, for when the travelers reached their western goals, the husbands still had to clear the fields and build the cabins and the wives had to spin and weave and make a home. The children, too, had the same tasks their predecessors had been saddled with two hundred years before. Of course, crude machines were slowly being invented to help in everyday work, but the basic, conservative threads of American family life were honored and firmly ingrained in American behavior. It was found to be a pattern that men and women violated at great risk.

This pattern proved so viable and productive that it prevailed through the end of the nineteenth century and well into the twentieth. In the 1920s, when I began to consider patterns of family life, I accepted the established form with never a question as to its efficiency as a way of ordering male and female relationships. I not only approved of what I saw but also became an ardent advocate of the system. My strong adherence to the traditional American family is curious, since during my early years I never lived in a house occupied by a husband or any other man. I was raised solely by women, and because I was aware of what I was missing I still feel that I was in some ways deprived.

Assault on the family as World War II begins. With the dislocations imposed by the war, including not only the shipment of our men to Europe and the Pacific but also the influx of women into the factory workforce, old patterns of life underwent such radical change that the traditional family was assaulted from every side. Indeed, well-authenticated data from the Census Bureau and other equally qualified sources present a portrait of family life today that is vastly different from what it was only a quarter of a century ago.

The number of divorced persons in the United States has nearly quadrupled, from 4.3 million in 1970 to 16.7 million in 1993, representing 9 percent of all adults aged eighteen and over in 1993. One study projected that of every thousand marriages that took place in the United States in 1985, 516 would end in divorce, with the wife and sometimes the children being abandoned. The proportion of men and women aged thirty to thirty-four who have never married has tripled since 1970. For women, the proportion has grown from 6 percent to 19 percent; for men, the proportion has increased from 9 percent to 30 percent between 1970 and 1993. Obviously, many American men have become afraid of marrying.

What is fueling the attack on the traditional patterns of family living can best be studied on three different levels, dictated by the ages of the participants. First is the radically changing sexual behavior of young people in the thirteen–twenty age group. Second is the altered courtship behavior of those in the twenty–thirty-five age group who are seriously looking for a mate. Third are the couples already married who face new problems in trying to keep their marriages functioning.

Assault on the family: the sexual behavior of youth. I am shocked when I read reports based on thorough research that many American children are engaging in sexual activity in their earliest teens or ·even at eleven or twelve. Government data in 1990 show that 41 percent of all teens aged fifteen to seventeen had experienced full sexual participation. This premature adventuring does not necessarily lead to a satisfactory later married life, and the practice has become so widespread that I doubt it can be reversed.

The persistent pressures of our society, especially those advanced by television and advertising, provide such a constant barrage of sexual images and suggestive behavior that young people are invited to start their sexual lives at increasingly younger ages.

The shocking advertisements of one manufacturer of blue jeans for adolescents were such blatant invitations to engage in sexual behavior that the public was vocal in its outrage, and the ads had to be discontinued. But others took their place, providing a constant show of sexual titillation.

Society has become almost indifferent to the fact that babies are born to thirteen- and fourteen-year-old mothers, and that young fathers accept no responsibility for the child rearing.

Teenage pregnancy has become so common that schools across the nation have found it necessary to offer special classes for high school girls and even grammar school girls who bring their babies to school. Today's young women beyond school age face no social ostracism if they have babies outside wedlock. Cohabitation is so common among all classes that illegitimacy naturally follows, and the added difficulty young women face in trying to find husbands makes it fashionable for women of strong character to have babies whether or not they have husbands. The insouciance with which attractive professional women have babies outside wedlock makes the practice seem almost the norm.

Of every thousand babies born in the nation, 326 will be to unwed mothers, and the babies will never know a father or become accustomed to a man in the household. Of the young girls who had illegitimate babies in 1994, 393,685, or 30.5 percent, were under the age of twenty. In 1994 there were 933 infants diagnosed with AIDS, and each year an estimated 5,000 babies are born with fetal alcohol syndrome as a result of alcoholism on the part of the pregnant mother.

Children's failure to receive any family discipline in the matter of having babies has inevitably followed upon the disintegration of discipline involving less complex problems. For some years I lived in an apartment house in which a spineless father and a weak mother ineffectually tried to discipline their feckless four-teen-year-old son. He started by shouting 'Shut up!' at his mother, and soon escalated to assertions that he would behave as he damn pleased. He began using such obscene language that another man who rented a room alongside mine suggested that he and I grab the kid and knock some sense into him. But I demurred: 'If we do that we could go to jail; if we touched him, his mother would leap to his defense.' So we listened in disgust, knowing that a modicum of discipline, gently but firmly administered, could have made all the difference.

Add to this lack of control at home the declining influence of our churches, the absence of discipline in our schools, the proliferation of gangs and the incursion into family life of drugs, alcohol and tobacco, and chaos is created in which it is virtually impossible for children to mature in a normal way.

One fact should be understood, and here I speak from an intense personal indoctrination: the claim that a child who grows up in a family with no father on the premises is somehow doomed to a life of ultimate failure condemns entire generations of children, especially those who are black, to malfunctioning lives and tragedy. What nonsense! I can point to scores of fatherless young people who have won enviable and secure positions for themselves. In an era in which as many as one fourth of our nation's children are being raised in single-parent homes, we are indeed fortunate that so many are able to overcome early adversities.

Since I was also fatherless, I saw firsthand the wonderful work that women can accomplish in raising adoptive children. From the beginning I was aware that I would have been better off had we had a father in our home, but when I saw how some husbands along our street behaved–drunken binges, physical attacks on their wives, brutal treatment of their children–I was grateful to have escaped that kind of parenting, although I retained my deep respect for the family as an institution, and still do. I am a family man, and I suppose my success as a teacher at all grade levels was a kind of sublimation of my desire for family.

Assault on the family: altered patterns of courtship and marriage. When Shakespeare dealt with the angst of young love in *Romeo and Juliet,* that tempest ended in a double suicide. It still happens today, as the dean of any large college can attest. Even if the threat of suicide is dampened, the psychological disturbance continues.

I do not take courtship traumas lightly. As a professor dealing with the young of marriageable age, I never lost sight of the fact that it was infinitely more important that the young student before me find a partner of the other sex with whom she or he could establish a lifelong association than it was to get an A from me. I still subscribe to that comparison of values.

My attitudes toward the changed patterns of courtship stem from a peculiar Pennsylvania background. In colonial days our Dutch farm families engaged in the custom of bundling, in which a young couple who were obviously serious in their intentions were allowed to conduct the next stages of their courtship while in a kind of bed, 'totally clothed or partially so, but separated at first by a stout board placed between them.' It was customary in those days for a wedding to be conducted only after the bride was pregnant. Of course by the time I came along, the formal practice had long since been discarded, but a kind of ipso facto bundling did take place among the local descendants of the old, so-called 'Dutch,' German families. It was orderly. It was more or less supervised. Pregnancies rarely ensued but promising marriages did. Having been familiar with such behavior, I was prepared for the 1960s radical revision of courtship patterns, but even so I was astonished when I heard that the twenty-one-year-old son of a strict Republican family had brought his nineteen-year-old girlfriend home for a weekend and assumed that she would share his bedroom. When I asked another member of the family how his parents had reacted to this type of courtship, she said: 'Mom and Pop ricocheted around the walls but they said nothing to Louis or Louise.' In our town, bundling had come full circle over a span of nearly three hundred years.

Couples are marrying somewhat later in life. The reasons for this are complex. The desirability of completing one's education and the increased importance of having completed at least some college work impose a delay in courtship and marriage. Also, the general difficulty of finding work at any level is a factor. And the prohibitive cost of housing frightens young people. Equally important is a change in what young people see as fashionable: a long and perhaps intimate courtship and a marriage in the late twenties.

Young women of marriageable age and eligibility are finding it difficult to meet marriageable men. I am perhaps influenced too much by two areas in which I have worked in recent years: Washington, D.C., and Austin, Texas. Because each is the capital city of a government staffed by successful men who are already married and hordes of unusually attractive young women in junior positions or working as secretaries, a normal marriage market does not exist. This means that many young women who are eminently suited for marriage do not find husbands, a sad loss for our society.

I have encountered a shocking number of fine young men who in former times would long since have been married (the pressures of society would have demanded it) who are today reluctant to commit themselves to matrimony. They tell me: 'I like girls but I've opted out of the marriage market. I have doubts about my ability to live peaceably with the new type of woman.' This is not mere verbalization with no substance; it is very real. My wife and I lived in two excellent locales near big cities in which many of the small farms in our district were occupied on a permanent basis by two men who were obviously content with that arrangement and intended to make it their lifelong preference. We liked the men and had friendly social contacts and felt easy with them. In my work in the arts I have been admirably served by young men who have decided not to marry, and I would be in a less favorable condition today without having had their help. But I am distressed by the fact that these men have removed themselves as potential husbands for the young women with whom I work. This self-imposed removal from the normal social mix means that quite a few young women will not find husbands. (This is another reason why such young women are increasingly willing to accept or even encourage motherhood without being married.)

And there is, off to one side and often no longer hidden in a closet, another group who are devising their own radically new definitions of what a family is. They are the homosexual men and the lesbian women who form solid attachments to people of their own sex and establish what they call families. Some are fragile arrangements of the moment, others as devoted to a lifelong commitment as a couple in a traditional marriage. They pose difficult problems for the general public, and most states have withheld from such unions the rights accorded to what people call 'real marriages.' Fights over how legally to classify the new arrangements will probably continue into the next century. Again, although I must view the loss of the traditional family with regret, it is undoubtedly in America's best interests to begin to become more tolerant—socially, politically and economically—of alternate lifestyles.

I have detected a profound and frightening change in the attitudes of young women and men toward one another. They seem, in recent years, to have adopted fierce adversarial stances, one against the other. Young men have grown afraid of young women they have found to be just as capable as themselves. The old sense of an easy companionship through the period of courtship has been converted into a tense battleground. I do not believe that an aggressive women's liberation movement is to blame; I

rather think it is some visceral reaction of men who feel their importance has somehow been attacked and diminished. I know
that I could never have dated a young woman who earned a
higher salary than mine, but I suspect that I am the slave of hide-
bound traditions. I do know, from what people of both sexes tell
me when I investigate their inhibitions, that young men today
face a much more difficult pattern of courtship than I did. In my
early years it never occurred to me that women had interests far
different from mine. I was a happy naïf.

(I recall an amusing cartoon, perhaps in *The New Yorker*, showing
a group of prehistoric women in the Lascaux cave, some of them
on a scaffold as they work on the newest mural of bison and
other creatures of the period. Says the master painter, a dumpy,
middle-aged woman, as she leans down to talk to her younger
helpers: 'Have you ever asked yourselves why it is there have
never been any serious male artists?')

I have sympathized with and supported the various movements of young women to gain an equal footing with men in the
educational and business worlds. I was a women's libber from
the start, utilizing a woman lawyer, a woman agent, a woman
editor, a woman publisher, a woman accountant and a woman
office manager, not to mention the endless series of women secretaries. At present I employ in one capacity or another four extremely helpful women, and if the female component had been
erased from my working life I doubt that I could have accomplished much.

My basic convictions are firmly held and will never change. I
was appalled when my adoptive state of Colorado revoked legislation that had assured the gay community equal rights, and I
applauded when a boycott was mounted against the state. I was
dismayed when various courts gave Irish patriotic and religious
marching societies the right to bar homosexuals from joining in

their Saint Patrick's Day parade. I wondered what Saint Pat would have thought of that!

Concerning the right of women to be Protestant or Catholic clergy I am ambivalent. I think that in the Catholic religion, the tradition of men-only priests is so powerful, dating back to the fulminations of Saint Paul, that its refusal to admit women to its clergy is understandable and perhaps forgivable. But I find it easy to accept a woman clergy in the Protestant churches. Indeed, the Presbyterian church that stands next to my home has a most admirable woman leader, and I believe her presence adds to that church's popularity and vitality.

In sports I believe that reasonable adjustments have been made. I'm delighted to see the strides achieved in women's basketball in our universities and find their playoffs for the national championships almost as exciting as the men's; and I wonder why professional women's teams have not prospered here as they have in Europe. I have known several superb women players who, if they wanted to continue basketball after graduation from college, have had to emigrate to Italy or to the surrounding countries in which women's leagues flourish and pay substantial salaries. I have awaited the formation of such a league in the United States but do not foresee that it is likely to happen in the near future.

On the simple matter of a young man and young woman finding each other and establishing a lasting union, a canny old cynic once told me: 'Marriage is a crapshoot.' It is a risk, but despite the sad condition in which half the marriages are today, the risk is still one of the noble gambles of the human race. And if the supposedly 'new' family that the right wing is sponsoring so heavily can partake of the common sense that has ruled our healthier families in the past, all the better, but we ought to move with caution before adopting a pattern that goes against the time-honored grain of American life. We must, however, begin to move because the traditionally societal mores surrounding courtship and marriage are changing.

Assault on the family: the problems of married couples. One would hope that when a couple has survived the passions of adolescence and the anxieties of finding a lifelong partner, the partners would be entitled to a blissfully relaxed last half of their lives. Not so, for that is when the storms often strike with the greatest fury. Some of the disruptions are so common and follow such clearly established paths that they become paradigms.

But before a discussion of the legal and political conditions that intrude on the later years of life and especially on marriages, let us look at the inescapable facts that face any couple whose members are both beyond the age of sixty. For nearly two hundred years the insurance companies of America have collected figures on human longevity. These data are reported in the actuarial tables that determine what rates a company must offer clients to ensure a reasonable profit on the transaction. If you are a white American sixty or over, this simplification of the tables tells you how many more years you can expect to live.

AGE	MALE	FEMALE	AGE	MALE	FEMALE	AGE	MALE	FEMALE
60	18.7	23.0	70	12.1	15.4	80	7.1	9.0
65	15.2	19.1	75	9.4	12.0	85	5.2	6.4

A white American man aged sixty-five will probably live 15.2 more years, but a white woman who has reached that age will probably live 19.1 years. So if their lives proceed in accordance with statistics, she can anticipate four years of widowhood. However, since men tend to marry wives younger than themselves, the period of probable widowhood is extended by a substantial number of years. Suppose that a man has married a woman five years younger than himself; when he is age sixty-five he has a probability of 15.2 more years; but his wife, who is then only sixty, will have a probability of 23 more years. She can look forward to eight years of widowhood.

There is, therefore, in the human equation so far as longevity is concerned, a marked advantage in being a woman, but this carries an obligation. She must prepare herself emotionally and financially for some years of widowhood. Now let us consider the nonstatistical factors that make the later years of life precarious.

One of the classic problems, and the most brutal, is the case of the capable young professional who, working hard for little pay, falls in love and marries. The early years of the couple's family life are idyllic. He is establishing himself in his career and she is helping; they are saving money, for she has helped him to pay off the debts he accumulated while getting his degree and building his reputation.

But now, in hundreds of cases across the nation, the husband is in his forties and a leader in his community. He associates with men his age who are like him professionally, but who married later young women who had been to college or who even had advanced degrees. His wife, who was so vitally important when he was being trained and establishing his credentials, has no advanced education, and day after day he sees painful evidence that she has not been able to keep up with him in his new life. He begins to see her as a drudge, a burden, as someone who is holding him back, and he divorces her so that he can marry an attractive woman who is highly educated and more socially adept.

I have observed at close quarters several such marriages and was appalled at the callousness with which the men disposed of their onetime helpmates, often leaving them without adequate funds to maintain a decent life. I have cheered when in recent years judges have begun awarding the abandoned wife substantial shares in the husband's accumulated wealth. I think of those decisions as American jurisprudence at its best.

Observers are apt to describe this situation, in which middle-aged men slough off their wives of many years in order to marry younger women, as a male mid–life crisis or, sometimes jocularly, as 'the male menopause.'

But women, too, will end marriages but for a different reason: they come to a point when they can no longer tolerate a bad marriage. There is a cartoon of a bewildered man telling a friend: 'I'm completely baffled. I thought we had a perfect marriage because in forty years she never once talked back. Then she up and walks out, still not sayin' a word.'

America's shift from being a producing society to a consuming one has had a destructive influence on family life. Husbands and wives alike, not only older couples who should know better but also younger couples enthralled by the idea of plastic money, have gone consumer–crazy with disastrous results: mounting debt, abuse of the credit card and its 18 percent interest on unpaid balances, wasteful buying of unneeded goods and, in some cases, the psychological destruction of the wife who becomes a shopping addict. Neighbors said of one woman who could not stop buying junk and charging it to her credit card: 'She's committing suicide by plastic poisoning.' Even children are vulnerable to this mania. Young girls must have clothes as good as or better than those of their friends; young boys insist on expensive basketball shoes as being vital to their self–respect.

When a newspaper carries the headline G.M.'S NEW DEVELOPMENT PLAN WOULD CUT 5,000 ENGINEER JOBS, terrible reverberations from that decision strike ordinary families that had probably not anticipated such a frightening turn in their family finances. Two consequences become almost inevitable: the husband can find only some job paying a near-minimal wage of five dollars an hour or even less, and the wife is driven to accept any kind of low-paying work. This means she will be out of the house most of the day. The obvious result is that their children become latchkey children who receive little supervision or discipline. Unemployment and underemployment have a devastating effect on all members of a family and often lead to divorce, and the phenomenon of the freewheeling child, usually a boy, who joins a gang is common even in middle-class suburban communities.

Because of research I had to do for my writing, I came to know three different married couples in their sixties in which the husband had behaved with a dignity and compassion I would not have believed possible. Each couple had occupied a position of some importance in our national life. One had been an ambassador to important nations, one had been the president of a large bank, one had been the president of a well-known university, and each had watched his wife, veteran of many years of happy married life, slip gradually into Alzheimer's disease. In each case the wife could not remember who her husband was, but she was convinced that she was in trouble because she believed he had stolen her money from her in a scam of some kind. The husbands never wavered. Remaining as true to their wives as on the day they took their marriage vows, they became round-the-clock nurses and companions and tried to keep in reasonable serenity the closing years of their lives. When you add the deaths of wives from cancer, husbands from heart attack and sons and daughters from AIDS, you realize that marriage is an institution that exists under cruel pressure.

And yet, in the numerous retirement centers in the nation, one finds many happy couples who are living together into their late eighties and nineties. They are beautiful to watch, for they are a reassurance to us all. Happy families can not only exist but also endure.

Assault on the family: the growth of nontraditional families. In recent years the stability of traditional family life has been threatened by the sudden growth of a custom that has existed on the edges of American life since Pilgrim days. It occurs when a man and a woman fall in love, but are wary of the confinements of a legal marriage. Aware of the radical step they are about to take, they decide to live together 'without benefit of clergy.'

The census figures on this trend, when combined with the results of several major research efforts, are staggering to an old traditionalist like me. One specialist reports that 49 percent of Americans between the ages of thirty-five and thirty-nine cohabit. Another study says that for people ages fifty to fifty-four the rate has constantly grown. The U.S. Bureau of the Census reports that of the nation's 93 million households, about 3.5 million consisted of cohabitants in 1993. These figures are far larger than I would have guessed.

At first glance they seem to threaten the family, but on closer inspection–and here I am reporting my own investigations–substantial families can result from cohabitation. There is a man, a woman and, in many cases, children. The partners are bound together by affection, not legalisms, and the children appear as stable as the children of divorced parents who find themselves with two mothers and two fathers. Carefully comparing the two conditions, one might easily conclude that except for legal difficulties, cohabitation is slightly to be preferred.

It is difficult for the purist to admit that the word *family* should cover cohabiting adults, but the majority of society appears willing to accept just that. Loving people living together in a stable union constitute a family, whether we approve of the idea or not. Does cohabitation threaten the old definition of family life? Yes.

Does it conform to the scientific definition of the word family? Yes. Do I recommend cohabitation? A qualified No, unless marriage would involve financial hardship. Do I respect it when it functions for others? An equally firm Yes.

Special problems arise when one asks that the word *family* also include unions of two homosexual men or two lesbian women. The best of these unions constitute a family in the extended sense of that word, and I have found no difficulty in accepting them as the equal of my own family.

What politicians must do and not do. It is not enough for me to catalog the ills that beset the American family; I must also recommend specific actions by our political leaders.

It is understandable, but nevertheless ridiculous, when our new congressmen and congresswomen preach that most of the ills of society can be cured by a return to the stabler family that assumed a responsibility for the proper training and education of its children. I must state, sadly and regretfully, that I do not think this can be done–the facts are that in 50 percent of all cases, a traditional family does not exist and has little chance of staging a comeback.

But with the resounding triumph of the young Republicans in the 1994 elections, we had an opportunity to change at least some of the old laws that worked against family stability and to pass new ones that gave married couples assistance. We may not be able to reverse the trend toward nontraditional families, but we *should* be able to provide assistance to couples who *do* desire the traditional forms of marriage, and I was heartened when the programs proposed by the new leaders of the nation clearly showed that they were strongly pro-family. But I was dismayed when the first bits of legislation they tried to enact were not so much a program to assist families but savage attacks on mothers and hurtful to programs that assisted babies and children. Their proposed legislation also suggested tax laws that penalized the poor and the middle class but provided tax bonanzas for the already rich upper classes.

When the barn-burning young Republicans and their religious right-wing leaders enthusiastically tout family virtues, they are really talking about discipline, adherence to a rigid morality, obedience to leaders and the stifling of any tendency toward intellectual exploration by either the parents or especially the children. My ideal version of the family, as I explained before, consists of a gathering of people around the dinner table discussing various topics and satisfying their intellectual curiosity. But I fear that the kind of family promoted by the extreme right will stifle the inquiring spirit that has animated American life. It is perhaps unfortunate, but reality dictates that we must accommodate nontraditional families. Rigidity of mind and suppleness of spirit do not go well together, and total reliance on the former tends toward dictatorship.

But I do grant that the young Republicans of Congress are right when they argue that remedial steps must be taken nationally to strengthen the family. They are also right that in the field of legal decisions more responsibility should be vested in the family and less in the hands of absentee governmental agencies. The useful steps that should be sponsored and enacted are these:

Clean up old income tax laws that penalize couples when they marry. This could be accomplished in a single session of Congress if the lawmakers put their minds to it.

Scrutinize the entire income tax structure to see where present laws penalize the middle-class family and divert tax advantages to the pockets of the already rich and favored classes.

Ensure that adequate funds supervised nationally by the central government are provided for the care of babies and children.

Provide national health insurance, and ensure that pensions already earned in Company A are transferable to Company B; the same transferability should be available in the field of health insurance.

Inspect and modify current laws governing both permanent adoption and temporary foster-home care.

When these essential improvements have been made, the government can attend to the more conspicuous manifestations of parental failure: criminal misbehavior of children; teenage pregnancy; dropping out of school prematurely; and gang membership.

I have been impressed by the good results the kibbutzim have had in Israel, where children have lived in community centers in which many families cooperate in sharing household chores, money management and the rearing and disciplining of children, but I cannot recommend such an institution in America because our traditions are so different from Israel's. However, I took seriously Speaker Newt Gingrich's early suggestion that America might consider placing abandoned children in what would amount to modern orphanages in which they could receive attention and develop good habits that would save them in later life. His proposal was ridiculed as soon as it was given a test run by the Speaker, but it was not dismissed by me, because it contained the germ of a good idea. Additionally, something like the old Civilian Conservation Corps could well be reinstituted with salutary results in salvaging youths who would otherwise be at risk. I would favor such an effort.

But inevitably any solution to the problems of the disintegrating family must hinge upon the creation of jobs or the imposition of some kind of system that would enable the very poor to gain some income so that they can spend the money to aid not only themselves but also the entire economy. Many will find this proposal distasteful, but the reality is that we must engineer some device whereby we can circulate money downward. The economic imperative, if we want to save the family, is to provide jobs of some kind for all. If the young Republicans and their allies on the Christian right are willing to confront this obligation I would support their battle cry that 'the family must be saved,' but if their program affects only unwed mothers and underprivileged children I see little chance for it to be effective. Under the bleak programs they have so far put forward I can see only the further destruction of the family. I refer specifically to their cuts in aid to depressed families, their almost brutal treatment of girls who become pregnant and their reduction of aid to children.

Recommendations

1. Congress and the state legislatures should sponsor laws that assist rather than punish the formation and security of family life.

2. Concomitantly, legislatures should nullify those indefensible income tax laws that penalize a man and woman who want to marry and form one taxable unit. Under our present laws the couples who marry suffer heavy tax penalties when compared with those who cohabit. My wife and I, cognizant of the fiscal penalties, advised such couples: 'Don't penalize yourselves by marrying. Just live together—you'll save a bundle.'

3. When the government lowers taxes, the couple joined in a good marriage should benefit, not the upper classes who already have as much money as they need.

4. State and federal laws should support families who seek to discipline their children in allowable ways. I deplore many of the

decisions handed down recently in which parents were penalized for administering totally acceptable discipline.

5. The courts should not prevent school authorities from disciplining their refractory students. Colleges and universities should also be encouraged by the courts to discipline their disruptive students, always provided that civil law, including the right of petition and review, is kept available to prevent arbitrary injustices. It is the job of the courts to establish the dividing line between discipline and individual rights.

6. No arm of government should be allowed to deprive couples living in the newer forms of union of their equal protection before the law. I do not advocate *special* considerations but I surely do defend an *equal* administration of the nation's laws.

7. Young men and young women should be encouraged to marry and establish a loving home. That is the millennia-old pattern for rearing children and it still beats any alternative.

8. Society should provide situations—clubs, recreation areas, church groups—in which young people can meet marriageable members of the opposite sex.

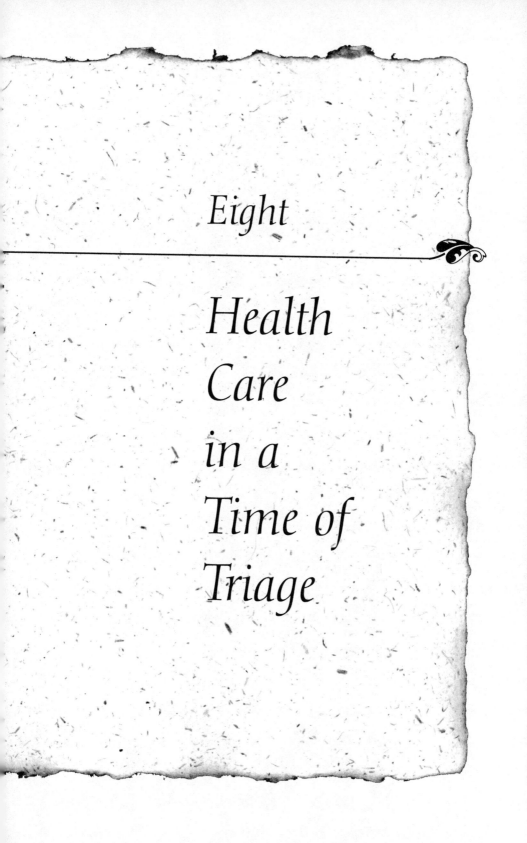

Eight

*Health
Care
in a
Time of
Triage*

*T*riage is a French word stemming from the root *trier*, meaning *to sort*. It was used originally in battlefield hospitals when the triage officer picked those wounded soldiers with the best chances of profiting from immediate medical care. Today triage is a word driving medical practice in the United States. Triage–type decisions are being made as to which type of patient is worthy of advanced medical care and which type has to be allowed to die. Triage–type decisions are being made as to what medical specialists a patient may see, what medical procedures and tests the insurance companies will pay for, and how many days a patient may remain in the hospital. Costs rather than needs are too often the determining factor for triage decisions.

The issue of triage today is complicated with many facets both rational and emotional. Let us imagine that we are members of a medical committee, meeting to consider how we would vote in two different situations. A hospital has one donor heart but two claimants who could use it. The first is a twenty–two–year–old mother with three children and a husband able to pay for the operation. The other is a seventy–seven–year–old with funds too skimpy to pay for a heart transplant. The choice seems too easy for our committee to discuss at length. The young mother gets the heart.

But now let's suppose the seventy-seven-year-old man is Albert Einstein, still working on his masterly explanation of the universe, while the young mother is an alcoholic who tests HIV positive and whose three children have inherited from her both the virus that causes AIDS and the negative effects of an alcohol addiction they acquired in the womb. Again, the committee requires only a few minutes to decide that Einstein gets the heart.

But triage decisions are usually not so simple. In a more realistic case, both the claimants are the same age, both are sterling citizens and both can pay for the operation. Now the choice requires an agonizing decision. Whichever way the committee votes may be justifiable but is nevertheless devastating for the loser.

I happen to know something about the procedures of triage because recently I chanced to see a confidential report on how best to use a healthy kidney that an automobile accident had supplied. The question was 'Which of our patients can profit most from this kidney?' Opposite my name were the notes 'Too old. Too many other medical problems.' In my case the decision was the right one. Other similar types of judgments are being made daily covering all sorts of medical problems. In the cases of transplanted organs, the deciding factors may be clear even if the solution isn't, but many of today's triage decisions in other less dramatic situations are based on the much more subtle factor of greed.

The United States is fast becoming a nation practicing triage on a grand scale. Unfortunately, greed rather than legitimate medical necessity has too often become the driving force behind triage. The share of our gross national product that we are currently willing to devote to medical services is being stretched to the limit. This means that such care as our nation is willing to pay for must be rationed financially; we can perform only so many costly operations in the hospitals, and we can provide only so many recuperative facilities and nursing homes. Our insurance companies believe that to protect their profits they should pay for only the most necessary (to *them*, not to the patients) operations and for limited specialized care. Hospitals, many of them profit-seeking corporations, charge fantastic rates for one day's occupancy of a bed, two thousand dollars being typical in some areas, and the costs of the advanced medical technology are astronomical. A huge number of our citizens cannot afford today's very expensive private health insurance and must receive their medical care in the emergency room of the local hospital. Much of the medical care for the indigent–say, the bottom fourth of the entire population–has to be paid for by government funds, and the costs to the taxpayer are becoming exorbitant.

Employers, both large corporations and small businesses, are deciding that, with the skyrocketing costs of medical care, the costs of adequate group health insurance now cut too deeply into corporate profits and are requiring their employees either to contribute to their health care costs or to join an HMO. The crisis is exacerbated by the fact that those who receive any kind of health care benefits from their employers cannot carry that insurance with them if they have to change jobs; we are the only major nation in the world that allows such a miscarriage of simple justice.

Any careful observer of America's health care system is perplexed as to why such an admirable collection of health experts, supported by one of the richest nations on earth, cannot provide *all* its citizens with an insurance system they can afford and with medical care through something like Medicare, now available only to elderly citizens over age sixty-five. Currently those under age sixty-five in the middle class are caught in the gap between the wealthy, who are able to pay high medical costs, and the very

poor, who receive some assistance through Medicaid. Our nation's failure to solve the problem of this gap is one of the mysteries of American life, especially when both the major political
parties agree that steps must be taken to solve it. The reason for
the failure is the rampant greed that pervades the medical profession, the insurance companies, the various types of medical
corporations and the character of the individual taxpayer.

I have been obliged to study American medical practice because my wife and I had five cancers to deal with, and I had a
massive heart attack, a quintuple bypass, the insertion of an electronic heart monitor, the insertion of a new hip and extended
treatment for kidney failure. In Pennsylvania, New York, Florida
and Texas, my wife and I had superb medical care. We saw American medical practice at its technical best.

But when it came to paying for the doctors and the hospitals,
we found ourselves in a jungle so insane that we could not even
guess who might have been sufficiently addled to have devised
it. The experience gave us an inkling of the tremendous waste in
our medical system. We both had Medicare, and my wife had
private insurance as well, but the government system was as
confusing as that of the private company. Both seemed to be
vying for a prize to see which could have the stupidest bookkeeping system and the most lost records. It was a draw.

Repeatedly I would receive itemized bills from doctors and
hospitals involved in some treatment. I would pay them
promptly, only to be told by the doctors that I should not have
paid so quickly: 'Wait till you get your check from Medicare and
then reimburse us for our services.' The next doctor would have
a different system: 'Ignore my bill. We get reimbursed by
Medicare for the portion they'll authorize, and then we bill you
for the difference.' Other doctors and other Medicare offices had
their own tricky systems; all seemed to be honest but inept.

We never protested the handling of our many cases, but preposterous tangles kept driving us to despair. I was most angered when, two years after I was sure I had paid everyone, I received a lawyer's letter warning me that if I did not pay his client's bill, which was now two years overdue, he would sue me in court for payment and inform the credit agencies of my delinquency. Upon checking, we found that indeed I had already paid the bill. The snafu that most angered my wife came when a kindly Medicare secretary told her they were sorry to hear that I had died. My wife could not convince them otherwise, and the system, having been defrauded by families who kept deaths secret to protect their relief checks, demanded from us a notarized assurance from our doctor and our bank that I was still living and that I had appeared in person in the notary's office to verify that fact.

If our experience with America's system of providing medical care was typical—and we heard of worse cases—the nation's insurance and medical bureaucracies are wasting billions of dollars on repetitive paperwork alone. With this type of waste, and with waste involving fraud, we citizens are legitimately angered by the unnecessary expenditure of our insurance, medical and tax dollars.

One of the truly serious matters that require immediate attention is the imminent danger of bankruptcy that threatens the entire Medicare and Medicaid system. Reliable predictions are that by the year 2002 there will be no more money in the Medicare fund unless sensible rectifications are made at once. This disaster will occur just as the baby boomers of the postwar 1950s are becoming eligible for payments from Medicare. Radical revision of the system is necessary, and Congress will have to act.

Apart from the Medicare agency, which has generally treated me well and generously, and apart from the technical proficiency, our medical system functions so poorly in many respects that it is a blot on our democracy. Its primary weakness–that it is not available to everyone at an affordable cost–would be easily corrected if we had the determination to act. Our deficiencies are not due to lack of knowledge; we know what we need to know. Nor do they represent the victory of one political party over another; all parties know the weaknesses that need to be repaired and have the desire to make things better. Nor is it a lack of medical knowledge; our training hospitals, our research laboratories and the qualifications of our physicians are unmatched. So what is lacking? We simply lack the resolution necessary to tackle the complexities of our health system and its obvious failure to serve the nation with maximum efficiency.

In the aftermath of the 1992 presidential election when Governor Bill Clinton of Arkansas was sworn in as president, I was relieved by his proposal to tackle seriously our nation's health problems. But I was shaken some weeks later when it became apparent that he would be installing his wife, Hillary, as manager of his medical program. It wasn't that I feared she might not be up to the task of being in effect a co-president in dealing with medical affairs, because she was a brilliant graduate of Wellesley College and Yale University Law School and a prime mover in Arkansas politics and social reform. I knew a good deal about her and assured my friends that she had an excellent chance of being our next Eleanor Roosevelt. The danger I saw was that our reactionary senators, congressmen, other political leaders and both men and women in the news media would not accept her and would be poised to vilify her whenever she gave them an opening because of some unwise statement or action. Within a few months her enemies had indeed nullified her effectiveness and discounted whatever good ideas she put forward.

But I did not anticipate the extent of the venom and the cleverness with which the insurance industry launched its television campaign against everything she proposed. Its Harry and Louise ads were as persuasive as any I have ever seen. This middle-class couple were so sincerely, so deeply worried about the health of the nation—and so eager to leave all decisions to the insurance people—that they made any allegiance to Mrs. Clinton's proposals seem unpatriotic. With a series of some five or six ads, each more manipulative than the ones before, they neutralized not only Mrs. Clinton but also the president. Any health plan the Clintons proposed would be dead on arrival. Their reforms never had a chance. They were not even voted on; they died aborning.

What is there in our national character that makes us incapable of tackling a relatively simple job like organizing and running an affordable national health system for all our citizens? Like so much of American life, the roots of this characteristic go back to colonial days, when, almost as an act of faith, the frontier family was supposed to stand by itself and look to its own members to safeguard the family. With doctors unavailable or in short supply, the frontier settlements usually had to struggle along for some years before medical services became available to their new communities.

When a doctor finally appeared in their midst, he was idolized and granted an exalted position that he may not have deserved. It was in this period that doctors came to occupy a position of power in community life. In my boyhood village doctors were trusted deities—so much so that I still feel that way about the doctors who treat me now.

At some point in the postwar period, American doctors became concerned about political threats to their incomes, and they declared war on any liberals who might pass legislation that would in any way curtail their unrestricted control over the fees charged for their services. In a campaign about which I can speak from personal experience they were joined by other workers in the health care field and by the insurance companies fearful of any type of regulatory controls. When I ran for Congress in 1962, word spread through the medical community that doctors could give my opponent, who despised any federal program in medicine, contributions of as much as $999 without the recipient's having to report the gift publicly. When the election was over, the local newspapers printed the lists of doctors who had each given my opponent the $999. The earlier report of nondisclosure had been an error, but the end result was that everyone knew that I was for public medical care and the doctors and my opponent were not.

Not surprisingly, American doctors have developed a hatred for the medical-system experimentation in Canada, where a relatively sound national medical program has been installed and flourishes. It resembles the great programs in European countries like Great Britain, Denmark and Sweden, and is in no sense radical. But the American doctors, terrified by what they saw happening in Canada, where the doctors no longer had unrestricted control over their fees, launched a program of vilification against everything the Canadian medical system accomplished. This was the period when any Canadian who had the slightest grudge against his national system could come south of the border and be assured of heavy newspaper coverage when he declared the Canadian system did not work and should be junked. In fact some 90 percent of Canadians liked their system and compared it more than favorably with ours.

The American Medical Association adopted, with equal success, the policy that had served the National Rifle Association so well. If any critic pointed out that every advanced country in the world except ours had a national health and insurance policy that worked, while we lagged behind, AMA apologists for our inferior system shouted that our system was better because we were a different kind of people who had a system that suited us perfectly—we had nothing to learn from Europe, whose people were effete and not as advanced as we were. The NRA has used the same argument when anyone points out that our murder rate from handguns is four hundred or five hundred times greater than the rates of civilized foreign nations: 'We're a different people with a unique history, so there's nothing to be gained in comparing us with what are essentially backward foreign countries.'

The sad part about our refusal to establish a sensible national program for health care is that we already have in place all the components required for such a system—components of the very highest caliber. From extended experience with doctors, hospitals, insurance companies and collateral medical agencies, I make the following evaluations:

Personnel: Our specialists, general practitioners and nurses are equal to the best in the world and, in many important specialties, superior. So they would be able to service any kind of delivery system we elected to install.

Hospitals: The ones in which I have been a patient have been superior, and for the most part the rest are excellent, but we appear to have so many superfluous ones that any less than excellent hospitals should probably be closed down.

Retirement centers: After I had seriously inspected some two dozen of the top installations, I reached two conclusions: living conditions, including exercise rooms and recreational areas, were excellent, but the health care facilities, so glibly advertised when attracting new clients, were almost always nonexistent. Much fakery is evident in this aspect of health care. You live in the beautiful condominium, but you are left on your own to find in the nearby town what turns out to be very ordinary health care.

Delivery systems: If a family has an income of more than eighty thousand dollars a year, its members can enjoy the best medical care in the world. Medicare is a precious boon even to such families, although they could probably exist without it, except in cases of catastrophic illness or injury.

Emergency care: People at the bottom of the economic ladder face a brutal task when trying to obtain adequate medical care. Persons without medical insurance use the emergency rooms for minor medical problems because they have nowhere else to go. No–charge emergency rooms are crowded, rushed and sparsely staffed. The waiting period is often intolerable. Other nations do better.

Nursing homes: They are almost universally deplorable. The health care they provide is often a farce, and anyone who can should avoid entry to such dead–end operations. There must be the occasional nursing home that does a respectable job, but I have never found it.

Transportation: Because transportation, especially the private automobile, is presumed to be easily available to all, home care from a physician or a nurse is usually unavailable. And if the family does not have a car, or if the one they do have is preempted by the breadwinner, the lack of transportation is itself a major medical problem. We do not handle this well.

Lack of universal care: We are the only major nation I know that does not provide its citizens with the assurance of universal health care. This deficiency is a scandal of which we should be ashamed.

Lack of lifetime insurance: Most major nations provide health insurance to all citizens, with the promise that it will follow them like a protective umbrella wherever they have to move in changing jobs. We should provide the same, but we lag far behind the other major nations in this respect. We have not been allowed to provide lifetime insurance because of the cupidity of the insurance companies, who fear government regulation and want to keep the monopoly for themselves, and the avarice of some doctors, who support and defend the insurance people. The insurance companies must continue to be involved in a new system guaranteeing lifetime insurance, and they must, of course, be allowed to make a reasonable profit, but they cannot be allowed to control the system. Private medical insurance can continue to be available for those who can afford not to trust a national system to meet all of their medical requirements.

Doctors' incomes: One of the most difficult alterations to make in our system will be the question: What is a just salary for the doctor, especially in days when budgets have to be rationalized? All signs point to two changes. Across the board, doctors' fee–for–service incomes will be under fire. Those with strong reputations, particularly the specialists in exotic fields, will be able to practice individually and will retain their yearly incomes of many hundreds of thousands of dollars. But the majority of their fellows will probably be forced to practice as members of group plans, under fee limits such as those imposed by Medicare. Doctors' incomes will be diminished, but I hope that equitable salary categories can be established; doctors *do* deserve good compensation for their skills, and we do not want to see our towns and cities filled with doctors who feel they have been cheated. Nevertheless, doctors will have to give up the idea of becoming millionaires on the backs of the taxpayers.

Cutting expenses: It stands to reason that in an age of triage, changes will have to be made in budgeting for Medicare (for anyone) and Medicaid (for the indigent), and some services now available will have to be rationed. Short of scrapping our current health care system completely and starting over with a bold new system of national health care, modifications to the current system *must* be made. The problem is: How can we police those changes so that fairness to all citizens is protected? Both political parties, Republicans and Democrats alike, know that some kind of limitation will have to be imposed on these two services, and although the word *triage* is rarely spoken, that's what the argument is about. And the subject is so vital to each party that the heated debate on medical costs has been at the forefront of the many disputed issues that have several times caused the government to shut down almost completely for weeks at a time, without any solution's having been reached. And the impasse could continue right through the rest of 1996 and dominate the presidential election in November. Health care is a major problem for our federal and state governments. Cutting expenses is obligatory if the system is to be saved, but it would be dangerous and unacceptable if billions of dollars were to be cut from Medicare services to the middle class and even more from the Medicaid services to the poor. This would be especially repugnant if the billions thus saved were used to provide the upper classes with a tax cut they do not need. That proposal seems so immoral that our nation should scornfully reject it, yet it is being seriously proposed.

In recent years a promising innovation in health care has begun to proliferate, the HMO (health maintenance organization), a sample of which can be located anywhere in the United States from small town to major city. It consists of a group of doctors and nurses–often assembled and managed by an outside corporation–who practice as a unit and offer to their communities a wide mix of medical services, but not procedures as difficult as heart transplants or brain surgery. For such cases they reach out to specialists in their area or in the nearest city.

The important word in the name is *maintenance*, the job of keeping you well. To enroll in an HMO the patient signs a contract in advance, paying a modest entry fee whether or not a doctor's services are needed at that moment. In most HMOs the patient is restricted to a choice among the doctors participating in his particular group. Any patient may, of course, consult with the doctor who had previously served as his family physician and pay him on the side for his help. But the experience of the ideal HMO is that the patient who signs up selects a doctor within the group who is found to be satisfactory.

By themselves the HMOs would not be a dominating force in the system, but they are backed up by guidance from a remarkable institution, Milliman & Robertson, a Seattle-based consulting firm specializing in medical economics. Milliman, roaring ahead in a field others had overlooked, quickly established itself as the arbiter not only of medical costs, about which it was an expert, but also of medical practice, about which it was formerly barely eligible to have an opinion. HMOs, insurance companies and hospitals seek guidance from Milliman on the most vital parts of their financial management. Because Milliman is not afraid to identify errors in medical practices and to issue guidelines to correct them, it has made itself the guru of triage.

Milliman's pronouncements, published as guides for the saving of money, are being accepted as law by insurance companies, HMOs and hospitals. In *The New York Times* Allen R. Myerson cited some of Milliman's edicts that have been widely adopted for patients under sixty-five without complications:

–You can't stay in the hospital for more than one day after a normal childbirth, or two days after a Caesarean. (This is being widely contested.)

–You can't stay in the hospital for more than three days for most strokes, even if you can't walk out.

–You can't have a coronary bypass unless the strongest drugs have failed to cure your chest pains.

Other consultants advise against hasty operations on the back, the prostate and the heart, and recommend that insurance companies cut back on the number of hysterectomies they allow.

The chief at Milliman and the authority in charge of the guidelines is Dr. Richard L. Doyle, a big, bearlike doctor, aged fifty-seven, with broad experience. He charges $395 an hour for individual counseling to hospitals and the like and his clients say: 'Worth every penny. He makes you do things you ought to have thought of by yourself.'

His directives seem to be clear–cut and in some cases brutally frank: Cut costs. Rationalize your procedures. Submit everything to close rational inspection. Cut out the frills. Make every medical process justify itself. Cut costs. He is adamant that patients stay out of hospitals as much as possible, and when they do have to go in, they should get out in a hurry.

The Milliman guides seem to work best on patients under the age of sixty-five; older patients have more complex problems and require more individualized care. Doctors with long experience to justify their more cautious behavior fight against the Milliman rules, but the hardest blow falls on hospitals, whose daily basic costs have exploded to an average of nearly two thousand dollars a day per patient. Wide enforcement of the Milliman rules by insurance companies will force many smaller hospitals to close, a result that many leaders in the health professions would applaud.

What we are witnessing is triage on a grand scale, but today's economic pressures and our unwillingness to pay the costs for national health care make its imposition inescapable. There are, however, certain illnesses that do not come under Milliman rules.

Patients with total failure of the kidneys, which as recently as 1970 proved fatal, can now be kept alive with better than 95 percent certainty. This is possible through a miraculous system called *dialysis*, funded for everyone by Medicare, in which waste products are removed from the blood and excess fluid from the body. This wonder treatment saves thousands of lives a year, and costly though it is, Milliman rules do not apply to it. You cannot shorten the time the patient must spend on the dialysis machine; it demands three hours a day, three times a week. Dialysis is an example of what can and should be done at the national level.

A man on dialysis asked me: 'Suppose Milliman or Congress decides to cut the number of dialysis machines by two thirds. Will the congressmen who vote for such an action agree to serve on their hometown triage committees: "*You* can have one of the chairs. Unfortunately *you* can't, so you must die"? I doubt it. Hard facts would supersede Milliman cost cutting.'

Fortunately, there are not many diseases like total kidney failure, so Milliman procedures have a possibility of reducing our national medical bills by an almost unbelievable amount, and I expect them to be adopted throughout the nation. At one time I was inclined toward recommending that HMOs expand their coverage in America, and for a while I thought I might join one. But when I announced this publicly I was greeted with loud protest and a recitation of several dozen horror stories. In fairness I must share a sampling.

The thoughtful doctor: When this doctor heard me speak favorably of HMOs he grew choleric: 'They're making robots of us doctors. Medical decisions of the gravest kind are being imposed by secretaries on the telephone. I had a woman patient with a severe complication that only an on-site examination and diagnosis could treat. I explained this, but the secretary with no medical training whatever told me: "Rules are, Doctor, that she gets one day in the hospital, and that's it." If I wanted to keep her for two more days, I could do it at my own expense or hers.'

The highly trained specialist in an exotic field: 'I'm embarrassed to say this, but there are not many of us in all America who are expert in this area of medicine. But when I advocated a somewhat unusual treatment for a patient with an advanced case, the girl on the telephone said: "Doctor, you know that's not authorized. Insurance does not cover that and your appeal is rejected." I was powerless, and I'm the expert with years of training, overruled by a telephone operator.'

A typical patient. 'I've paid my entry fee and been on the rolls for seven months and have not yet been able to schedule a meeting with my primary health care provider. I have a feeling we're being treated like cattle.'

A typical family physician of superb reputation: 'I've been forbidden to recommend to any of my patients that they consult with a specialist in some field in which I'm adequate but not really well informed. To save pennies they invite serious setbacks that will cost thousands.'

Because of this constant drumbeat of criticism, I have become wary of placing too much power in the incestuous relationship of insurance companies and HMOs as a solution to our medical problems. Are the Milliman rules turning doctors into robots? Or are the protests of the doctors merely self-serving laments for the simpler–and more profitable–doctor-patient relationship of yesteryear? Are those days not doomed by the computer, which can handle diagnosis so ably, and by the Milliman rules, which show the health care profession how to save money? After painful attention to what is best for the country, I must vote against the HMOs as dictatorial, self-aggrandizing and indifferent to the welfare of the patient. Their abuse of doctors disqualifies them, and I see them now as a clever mask to perpetuate the tyranny of the insurance companies. The persuasive grain of truth in the otherwise absurd Harry and Louise advertising blitz was that we *do* fear having the medical decisions, so crucial to our very lives, being made by HMO secretaries and telephone operators rather than by doctors. There must be a better way.

But just as I am awakening to the dangers of the HMOs I learn that Congress is thinking seriously of using them as the basis of our national health care system. They and the insurance companies will dictate to patients, doctors and nurses how they shall operate. Saving money will become the rule in American health. I must protest against this unwise and brutal decision. The insurance companies' profit margins cannot be the driving force behind what is and what is not adequate medical care, and neither should the profit margins of organizations such as the HMOs be the decisive factor. The motive for our medical care system has to be the health of our citizens rather than the health of a financial statement.

One test of any health care system is how it functions in a disaster or reacts to the sudden onset of a plague or an epidemic. In 1995, when the government building in Oklahoma City was destroyed by a massive bomb explosion, the health agencies of the area responded instantly and with the most admirable precision to save the lives of those few who survived. Praise was heaped upon the doctors who reacted so spontaneously to the call for help. Special accolades went to the medical team that dug deep into the rubble, which might have fallen on them at any moment, where they worked in darkness to amputate the leg of a woman trapped under a heavy slab of concrete that could not be moved. We have grown to expect doctors and nurses to do their best under the most perilous circumstances, which, as in the case of Oklahoma City, they invariably do.

But I am less impressed by our national response to plagues. These are unexpected eruptions of some unfamiliar death-dealing affliction like the spread of leprosy in Old Testament times, or the outbreak of the ancient plague in the London of 1665, or the strange attack of cholera among those journeying westward on the Oregon Trail in the 1840s, or the deadly pandemic outbreak of influenza in 1917. In the United States our medical system is currently engaged in fighting two modern plagues, and the battle reports are not encouraging.

AIDS: One of the perplexities facing health care administrators is: 'How should HIV–positive patients who can be expected to contract full-blown AIDS with its threat of early death be treated?' AIDS must be handled as an epidemic that strikes across our entire population. That it has been associated in the media with homosexual behavior is only partly accurate; AIDS is also attacking the general population. (Indeed, the rates of increased cases are greatest among heterosexual young women.) We should fund research to identify and distribute cures to halt the HIV infection but also provide hospices in which AIDS–afflicted people can die with dignity.

Tobacco: Two aspects of our health program are so perverse they defy rational explanation. Since 1964, when the famous report of the surgeon general launched an attack on the health hazards of cigarette smoking, our federal government has aggressively campaigned against tobacco. Advertisements for cigarettes could not appear on television. Packages in which cigarettes were sold had to carry a government warning that they were hazardous to one's health. Taxes were piled on cigarettes, and laws were passed forbidding people to smoke in public places. Millions of families posted PLEASE DO NOT SMOKE signs in their homes, and many public buildings such as libraries, hospitals and entire colleges and universities became nonsmoking areas. In addition, scientists were remorseless with their barrage of studies that proved to the satisfaction of the general public that cigarette smoke by itself was carcinogenic if the nonsmoker inhaled enough secondhand smoke. Millions of two-pack-a-day smokers quit.

But while this government campaign was gaining new converts every month, our Congress was nullifying the effort by kowtowing to a powerful group of southern senators and congressmen who demanded that the government continue to protect the tobacco industry; the law even paid southern farmers subsidies to cultivate and market their tobacco crops. This bifurcated policy—condemn cigarettes but subsidize farmers to keep on producing huge surpluses—left many Americans bewildered, for they saw that they were paying twice for the cigarette: once when it was produced with a subsidy and a second time when hundreds of thousands of men and women contracted lung cancer and emphysema, leaving behind massive medical bills that often had to be paid from government funds.

The insanity of our tobacco policy was exacerbated when we exported our tobacco abroad and made it attractive for foreign governments to import our cigarettes and to endanger their own people. This three-pronged policy—condemn the cigarette at home, do everything to diminish its use within the United States, but pay farmers a subsidy so that their tobacco can be both marketed at home and shipped abroad to other nations—is a social crime with international reverberations.

This behavior on our part of forcing tobacco on other nations is reminiscent of the opium conflict of 1839–42, in which a powerless China sought to halt a nefarious opium traffic that was enervating her people but was defied by Great Britain, which earned a huge profit from the opium trade. Britain initiated what is known as the Opium War, and was joined by other European nations. The result was the imposition of duty-free ports along the China coast inhabited and controlled by foreign powers. The United States participated in this shameful incident, and opium continued to be forced upon the Chinese.

I shall not belabor the analogy except to point out that for the last one hundred fifty years foreign historians have condemned Great Britain for her reimposition of the opium traffic upon a nation that did not want it.

To summarize, the components of a world-class medical system are already in place in the United States. What has been lacking so far is a firm resolve to pay the costs of welding the pieces together into a workable pattern that will meet the nation's needs. I doubt that this can be achieved if we allow the insurance companies with their special interests to dictate what form that system will take.

I find it intolerable that our political leaders, those in charge of our plan of taxation, should propose a solution that would leave an enormous minority at the bottom of our economic ladder without reliable care or the insurance backing to acquire it. Other civilized countries have national systems of medical care to benefit all citizens, but the citizens are taxed to pay for it. Americans must be brought to realize both that medical facilities *must* be made available to all and they will be taxed to pay for them.

I consider health care to be one of the four most important issues on the national agenda. Not in order of priority they are: race relations, getting money to the dispossessed, education and health care. For me, improved race relations are a philosophical-moral imperative; helping the people at the bottom of the ladder is an economic necessity; education is vital if we are to continue to compete in world markets; health is a matter of life and death for all of us.

Recommendations

1. Our national health care system must be made rational and all participants must bear their share of the costs.

2. It must include care and insurance for all citizens.

3. Medicare and Medicaid should be continued, but savings must be made in each agency.

4. The horrible mess of government paperwork in the health care field, especially in Medicare, should be simplified.

5. If changes currently proposed are implemented, doctors could become like schoolteachers: everyone will acknowledge the important role they play but will be reluctant to pay them a respectable wage. We must not let this happen. Multimillionaires, no. Decently paid public servants, yes.

6. The nation seems destined to move toward an HMO system. But before that happens, the current dictatorial tendencies of HMOs must be curbed.

7. We must stop subsidizing tobacco, restrict its use here at home, and cease our export of it to other lands. In the year 2030 our country might well be cited in some international court for such near-criminal behavior.

Nine

*Our
Macho
Society*

*M*acho is a Spanish adjective meaning 'male.' It would be improper to say: 'He has *macho*,' for the noun is *machismo*. To say 'He has *machismo*' would be proper usage, but in contemporary English the word *macho* has come to mean excessive or posturing male characteristics. The United States as a nation of active people has veered, I believe, toward a macho image of itself, and this is having an effect on many aspects of society. Macho ambitions explain, for example, why football has superseded baseball as our national pastime and why control of guns seems an impossibility. Among the deplorable effects of machismo in America are the complete degradation of many of our legitimate sporting programs, the ever-increasing numbers of children murdered by handguns, the rise of vicious militia organizations, the proliferation of vitriolic and dangerous radio and TV talk shows, and the depictions of violence in motion pictures that make violence appear to be a norm in life.

The seed of this emphasis on near brutality in American life was germinated far back in colonial times, when a man's merit was judged by his ability to stand against all opposition in his community. He must subdue the land, defend his family and himself against danger and, when challenged by the local bully, stand up and fight. Even frontier sports for amusement could be very rough. Fistfights were bare-knuckled and often fought to the complete exhaustion of one or both fighters; wrestling condoned gouging and punishing holds that would later be outlawed. The legacy of such exhibitions was a glorification of violence and the implanting of a belief that violence was a proper yardstick by which to judge a man and his games.

But the influence of violence went beyond sports and established a norm for many aspects of American life. Political battles could be rowdy affairs and laws were apt to be draconian. In many locales the lynching of blacks became widely acceptable, and local posses often dispensed vigilante justice, including the death sentence.

One of the most revealing measures of the influence of macho imagery in American life is the degree to which the macho vocabulary of sports has come to dominate our thinking in politics, business, recreation and general conversation. A whole new vocabulary has evolved, a kind of shorthand for conveying thought in a host of situations:

> Senator Dole delivered a knockout punch to Pat Buchanan.

> Microsoft has hit the opposition with a slam-dunk, in-your-face move.

> Both sides must have access to a level playing field.

> For the Democrats it's always fourth down and nine to go.

> In the debate the opposition scored nine unanswered points.

> In its negotiations with the British, American Airlines is playing on a sticky wicket.

The media and sports conduct a symbiotic affair. There is a powerful relationship between newspapers and the professional sports; television, of course, exists in large part on its endless parade of spectacular regular–season games followed by the cluster of playoffs in hockey, basketball, baseball and football. The relationship between television and football is almost mystical; one seems to have been invented to support the other. Several national magazines concentrating on sports thrive while those specializing in the arts barely survive, and those magazines emphasizing serious thought, including politics, gain only limited numbers of readers. With its pocketbook our nation has established its priorities in entertainment and popular culture: sports gain the most and the arts relatively little. At the end of each season our presidents even feel obligated to invite that year's championship teams to the White House; our political leaders are well aware that Americans love their sports heroes above all other performers.

We rarely give thought to the powerful influence by which sports, with its macho mentality and vocabulary, dominate many aspects of our national life. Years ago Lewis Terman, a noted psychologist who devised the first I.Q. test, made an interesting comparison between the U.S.S.R. and the United States. In the Ukrainian city of Odessa near the Black Sea, a genius in teaching the violin, Leopold Auer, operated a center that produced many notable violinists imported by the world's symphony orchestras as their first violinists. The truly superior young men like Jascha Heifetz, Mischa Elman, Efrem Zimbalist, Toscha Seidel and Michel Piastro became world–class soloists. Terman went on to say that during the same period we in America instead revered sports above all else and produced champion boxers like Jess Willard and Jack Dempsey, baseball players like Honus Wagner, Christy Mathewson and Babe Ruth. Terman accurately concluded that a nation revealed its priorities by the way it nominated its heroes.

Another index of how our nation evaluates its citizens is to check on whom we elect to Congress. Jack Kemp was an excellent football quarterback for the Buffalo Bills who retired and ran successfully for Congress in New York. Bill Bradley was a sensational basketball player for Princeton and the New York Knicks who then easily won election and reelections to the Senate. Jim Bunning was a perfect-game pitcher for the Phillies, among others, and retired from baseball to become a U.S. congressman from Kentucky. Tom McMillen was a sterling basketball player for the Atlanta Hawks and the Washington Bullets, who went on to become a congressman from Maryland. Steve Largent, a football Hall of Famer who played for the Seattle Seahawks, became a congressman from Oklahoma. Ralph Metcalfe, an Olympic sprinting champ, became a congressman from Illinois.

In the same period, every one of the handful of writers who ran for major office was roundly rejected: William Buckley and Norman Mailer for mayor of New York; Gore Vidal in New York for the House of Representatives and in California for the U.S. Senate; and I for Congress from Pennsylvania. When I ran, the rumor which was circulated that you can't trust writers because they're all socialists or worse appeared to confirm the generally poor opinion about writers and all other artists. None, so far as I know, has ever won a major public office.

A marvelous football star I knew in one of the big Western universities exemplifies an aspect of the macho attitude that pervades college athletics. I shall call him Dooby Kane, a defensive back with unbelievable skill whose college career I followed with more than usual interest. I was gratified when he was nominated for All-American, but I was less pleased over the rumors that kept reaching me, such as: 'This guy Dooby is a world-class hell-raiser.' I learned that the athletic department of his university kept on its payroll a lawyer whose job it was to protect the team's football players who ran afoul of the law: 'If Dooby gets a traffic ticket, Mr. Benson's on hand to ask the police to quash it; Dooby is needed on Saturday and mustn't be aggravated by a silly thing like this traffic ticket.' The athletic department's lawyer moved in even on charges of rape and paternity cases and kept the football players free of annoyances. Dooby Kane lived in a fairy-tale meadowland in which nothing hurtful or unpleasant could touch him.

Even though I recognized this legal service was not doing Dooby any good in the long run, and even predicted that at some later point reality would overtake him, I was nevertheless delighted when one of the top Pacific Coast teams in the National Football League made Dooby its first-round choice after his graduation. He deserved it, and I watched with a sense of 'I told you so!' when he made the first team and performed with his customary brilliance in the opening series of games.

At that point I lost track of him, satisfied that he had successfully made the leap from college to the professionals, but much later, while working in Europe, I chanced to see a stateside newspaper with shocking news: Dooby Kane, on his way to being rookie of the year, had been arrested in California for the after-game rape of one of the cheerleaders. Now, however, in adult life, there was no longer a lawyer paid to shield him from trouble, connive with the legal authorities and persuade the young woman to withdraw her charges. Dooby Kane was sentenced to three years in jail, his once glorious career in tatters. The college athletic system had taught Dooby that his athletic abilities made him immune from the consequences of his actions; he learned too late that there *are* consequences for crimes against others and against society, even a society that worships his abilities.

I spend much time these days studying early civilizations and pondering where it was that some made the fatal mistakes which led to their loss of leadership in their worlds; while some powers soared to great heights, others sank into obscurity. Such speculation leads inescapably to ancient Greece, about which we have a more complete documentation than we possess, for example, about Charlemagne's medieval France.

In ancient Greece the most powerful state was Sparta, which opted for a militaristic society in which soldiers and generals reigned supreme. In the beginning Sparta dominated the other Greek city-states; her militaristic principles were sound and effectively employed in a series of wars, invasions and realignments of power. For long stretches of Greek history it seemed as if Sparta would prevail.

But in another part of the Greek peninsula another city founded on gentler and more thoughtful precepts was rising. In time Athens, largely forswearing military conquest, became the home of philosophers, playwrights, historians and artistically minded rulers who sometimes resembled kings but at other times were merely outstanding private citizens who possessed an aptitude for governing.

Gradually at first and then precipitously, mighty Sparta crumbled, its emphasis on military solutions to problems having dissipated its vitality and capacity for confronting new challenges. Sparta's power vanished and it became a bleak reminder of a theory of government that went badly wrong. Athens, with its noble traditions of art, drama, philosophy and speculation as to what constituted good government, still thrives as a major European capital. More important, the precepts of Athens constitute one of the major illuminations of the human mind in the Western world.

Sparta can be accurately described as a macho society, one in which the so-called manly virtues were at first extolled with impressive results but then were finally revealed for the barren philosophy they really represented. Athens was by no means a weak, effeminate counterpart to tough, masculine Sparta; it was far too rich and too varied, and too willing to speculate boldly on alternatives to its government and its society, to be so categorized. It was what might be termed a city–state in the humanist tradition– a democratic society. It did not prove that the pen is mightier than the sword; it often had to fight for its existence. But when peace was restored it returned to its philosophy and art. Sparta elected a lifestyle doomed from the start; Athens discovered an alternative, one that men and women through the centuries and around the world would seek to re–create in their nations.

I have a strong suspicion that the United States is surrendering to a macho style of society and government. We are transforming ourselves into a modern Sparta, and if we continue careening down that path we will end in ruin. The nations in the next two hundred years that can re–create the values of Athens will survive in quiet grandeur while the new Spartas will duplicate the tragedy of the original and become arid spots on the world map.

I have several observations to support my likening of our society to macho Sparta. Our addiction to sports is as intoxicating as it was to the Spartans and, as I've said, today dominates television, the daily press and social discussion. The examples I gave earlier of the proliferation of a sports vocabulary as a substitute for logical or precise thinking can be multiplied. Our excessive preoccupation with games is self–defeating in that it does not lead to thoughtful discourse, and our excessive reliance upon the sporting idiom even suggests that we have adopted the macho sporting experience as a summary of our major values. To do so cheapens the discussion of values in a moral life and lessens the options of our political leaders.

In no other aspect of our national life is the tyranny of sports more destructive than in our educational system. I am personally deeply indebted to sports; they rescued me from years of deprivation and helped me go to colleges and universities. I attribute much of the resilient good health I enjoyed for many years to the basketball I played till age forty and the tennis that I stayed with into my early eighties. And I also am a sports fan–I would never miss the Final Four basketball championship games on the tube.

So I do not denigrate the positive contributions of sports, but neither do I condemn lightly its negative influences. When in the town in which I used to live, boys in grades one through four are organized into peewee leagues while their sisters are still restricted to being trained to be cheerleaders, something is clearly out of balance.

In the next grade level, five through eight, the games become far too serious, and high school coaches prowl the Friday–night contests to spot the superior fourteen–year–old athletes they can invite to attend their high schools. The chicanery of managing young athletes begins at this level and will continue till the boy is a young man of twenty–six or twenty–seven. I concede that many of the young derive, as I did, positive benefits from the experience. But I am even more aware that many more of the boys are chasing a will–o'–the–wisp; only a charmed few will achieve profitable careers with the professional teams.

From what I've heard on the various campuses with which I've been associated, even the term 'scholar–athlete' has become an oxymoron; I judge that the average player entering a college or a university will have acquired by the end of his fourth year of playing for his school the equivalent of only two years of academic work at the most.

In any number of large universities, the chancellor's salary is a fraction of the many hundreds of thousands that the football or basketball coach earns from his salary, television appearances and advertising endorsements. This is so out of balance that no sensible observer can think it is rational.

A very macho aspect of the average university's athletic program is the preposterous manner in which it handles women's
athletics. I studied one school that had a student body divided
exactly 50–50 between men and women, yet only $250,000 of the
yearly sports budget of $4 million was allotted to women's pro-
grams. This disproportion was justified on the basis that men's
football and basketball were 'real' sports that brought in large
funds, while girls' games were just that: pleasant frolics that no
one took seriously. When I first wrote about this I asked: 'Where
does the administration think that babies come from?' The health
of women is certainly as important to society as the health of its
young men, and I suspect that women's health might be even
more important. Even so, as a realist, in an effort to placate the
coaches I would probably, if I were president of a university, approve of a budget giving men's athletics a larger split than the
women, perhaps proportionate to the revenue men bring into
the university. It is true that men's basketball and football do
bring in considerable revenue and therefore deserve some ac-
commodation.

When our federal government enacted a law, Title IX of the Education Amendments of 1972, requiring all colleges and universities receiving federal aid to provide their women students with
athletic facilities and scholarships comparable to the men's, the
macho men who governed athletics on the various campuses devised a score of clever moves that enabled them to more or less
ignore the new law. And, when they grudgingly did make some
concessions, a cruelly unfair situation developed. As soon as it
became clear that the women coaches of girls' teams were going
to receive substantial salaries and the administrators of the
women's divisions would receive proportionate funding, men
began to appear as chairmen of the women's programs, and
younger men became coaches of the girls' teams, especially bas-

ketball and volleyball. For many years Title IX remained ineffective, particularly after male coaches in several schools began to deride women's programs as: 'bikes for dykes,' a brutally disparaging put-down.

I must temper my remarks by explaining that I had a favorable introduction to Title IX at the University of Texas, which had enjoyed one of the most sensible and mature programs for women. Under the sage administration of Donna Lopiano, who went on to become the executive director of the Women's Sports Foundation, and with the coaching brilliance of Jody Conradt, Texas fielded women's basketball teams that went undefeated through long seasons, capturing national championships en route. I was a big supporter of those teams and those coaches, and had Title IX been as equally honored on all campuses the scandal of women athletes' being denigrated and cheated would not have occurred. Because of Donna Lopiano's determination to win just rights for her women, conditions are marginally better now, but the struggle goes on.

Not only does sport dominate much of our national life, it is becoming more violent. I recall the National Football League's sale of a videotape consisting of near-lethal collisions when three-hundred-pound tackles smashed into running backs weighing two hundred fifty. The viewer was numbed by the violence, and I later observed that the league finally stopped showing the tape; it was too brutal to represent what was supposed to be a game. In the broadcasting of sports events, however, emphasis is still given to massive collisions. The often-used shot of two rams with enormous horns smashing into each other seems to serve as a paradigm for how humans should behave. Men's ice hockey with its extravagant brutality (much of it staged, I suspect) is finding a growing audience and new arenas in the American South–Miami, Tampa Bay, Dallas–for its preposterous machismo. When I wrote my book on sports in America twenty years ago I refused to take either boxing or ice hockey seriously because, as I told my editor: 'I'm pretty sure hockey with its staged brutality will fade away before long. The public will reject the gladiator approach.' I also predicted that if basketball didn't clean up its act it would lose customers. How wrong I was! Hockey has not only expanded into ever-widening markets but has even lured men's basketball into putting on spurious clashes between its giant players. Ten years from now there will probably be ten more cities with hockey or basketball teams. So much for my crystal ball. America's macho exhibitions make the bottom lines of the year-end financial reports tingle with the clink of cash. We want our sports to be violent and, as we have seen, this desire stems from a long tradition of violence in many aspects of American life. Our macho attitudes toward violence are making of us a Sparta rather than an Athens.

While working on this segment I noted how news about three representatives of our macho society dominated TV coverage of national events. First, the O. J. Simpson trial fascinated the public. Although the majority of people reported to the pollsters that they believed him guilty, many also believed he should go free because he was, after all, a charismatic football hero. Second, the media devoted tremendous amounts of space to Duke Snider and his pleading guilty to tax fraud; the public was willing to forgive him because he was a baseball Hall of Famer. Third, the African American community of Harlem in New York City planned a gala celebration honoring the boxer Mike Tyson, and the leaders of the area eagerly volunteered not only to participate in the affair but also to lead it. Those TV messages involved a football player who was a confessed wife beater, a baseball player who was an admitted tax evader and a boxer who spent three years in jail on a rape conviction. What does the nomination of these three as American heroes and role models reveal about our value system?

The most instructive proof of our nation's increasingly vigorous move toward a macho society can be seen in our unique fascination with guns, our insistence on having them and our willingness to accept murder as a result of the huge number we allow and even encourage private citizens to own.

Bob Herbert, a columnist for *The New York Times*, in his Op–Ed piece for March 2, 1994, offered some shattering statistics: 'In 1992, handguns were used in the murders of 33 people in Great Britain, 36 in Sweden, 97 in Switzerland, 128 in Canada, 13 in Australia, 60 in Japan, and 13,220 in the United States.' We are the murder capital of the world; most of our killings are done by persons using handguns. Herbert continued with other astonishing data: that one year's total of 38,317 citizens killed by firearms was more than the total number of American troops killed in battle in the Korean War.

In American history the weapon of choice has been the handgun in attempts to assassinate U.S. presidents. Here is the record:

1865: President Abraham Lincoln shot to death by John Wilkes Booth.

1881: President James Garfield shot to death by Charles Guiteau.

1901: President William McKinley shot to death by Leon Czolgosz.

1963: President John F. Kennedy shot to death by Lee Harvey Oswald.

In addition, in 1933 President-elect Franklin Roosevelt was nearly murdered when a bricklayer named Giuseppe Zangara shot at him but killed Mayor Anton Joseph Cermak of Chicago instead. In 1950 President Harry Truman was shot at by Puerto Rican radicals. President Gerald Ford was shot at twice in 1975 by deranged women, and in 1981 President Ronald Reagan was nearly assassinated by John Hinckley, Jr.

This is a record of shame that no other civilized nation can even approach. The national outcry against the killing and the near misses has not been sustained; it has been tempered by absurd claims that a loss of our rights to own handguns, even machine guns, might destroy the U.S. Constitution. One is tempted to conclude: 'Americans are willing to have their presidents murdered if it means that citizens can keep their guns. It's a risk that goes with the job.'

The data just cited regarding the proliferation of guns in our country and our record of assassinating our presidents, let alone such distinguished citizens as Martin Luther King and Bobby Kennedy, can perhaps be explained by the fact that we remain a frontier society. When I lived in Pennsylvania, Massachusetts or New York, I could not understand the American passion for guns, but when I lived in Colorado and Texas I saw that otherwise sensible men could have monomaniacal fixations on their firearms. To a man in Wyoming or Montana, a gun is an entirely different weapon from what it is in Pennsylvania. In the western states it is a badge of honor, a memorial of the good old days when men defended their isolated homes against the threats of the wilderness. Their firearms are the ultimate proof of their machismo. I knew ranchers who confessed that they would give up their wives rather than surrender their guns. I also watched as they became fanatical supporters of the National Rifle Association and relied upon it as the protector of their rights as a man.

The National Rifle Association, with its brilliant public relations, is one of the prime forces in establishing and augmenting
our devotion to the gun. After the 1994 election it issued a handsome pamphlet showing on one page the portraits of thirty-two
politicians who had dared to vote for gun control, and on the
second page the same thirty-two portraits, each stamped across
the face with a red-letter DEFEATED.

If you doubt the power of the NRA I suggest that you write for
a copy of their *Ten Myths about Gun Control*, a twenty-nine-page
pamphlet that brilliantly rebuts every argument put forward
against guns or advocating their control. The writing is first-rate,
and the possession of a gun is equated with patriotism. There is
an amusing argument that the 87 gun murders in Japan in 1990
are really equivalent to the 10,567 killed in the United States. Further, the proliferation of guns in our country has nothing to do
with the murders; the murder rate is merely a difference between
national cultures.

I hear the same arguments from the gun owners I know. If I try
to recite the appalling statistics on accidental deaths from gunfire, they counter with statements difficult to refute: 'Guns are the
American way. They differentiate us from weaker nations like
France or Belgium.' By implication the speakers reveal that they
think the difference lies in the historic fact that we honor the existence of a macho ideal, while other nations do not.

From such experiences I have concluded that there is nothing
we can do to staunch the bloodshed caused by the gun. As a nation, too many of us want it that way. We want any citizen other
than a criminal already in jail to have the right to own an automatic crowd-killer that can mow down patrons dining peacefully
in a McDonald's hamburger joint (twenty-one dead) or a Killeen,
Texas, cafeteria (twenty-three dead).

There have been too many 'hunting' accidents. In Maine a wife
went out into her own backyard wearing white mittens. A hunter

saw the flash of white and, concluding he had a deer in his sights, blazed away and killed her. When the gunman was belatedly brought to trial, the Maine jury refused to find him guilty: 'It was her fault. She should have known better than to wear those white gloves.'

At the bottom of my lane in Pennsylvania, a child waiting for a school bus was shot to death and the hunter's excuse was: 'He moved, didn't he?'

Sometime later I was sitting at my desk in my house at the top of the hill when a phone call came that took me to another room. In my absence from my desk, a hunter saw a reflection in my window and, thinking it was a deer, fired two bullets through my window. Had I still been sitting there, I would have been murdered.

There were other shooting incidents that were more chilling because the killing was intentional. While working on a manuscript in Miami I became aware that my daily newspaper was carrying a sequence of stories that were almost identical with this one: 'Rafael Lopez, football star and straight-A student at Wellover High, was shot to death in chemistry lab by a fifteen-year-old boy who felt that Lopez did not pay him adequate respect.'

When I started to ask about these killings during school hours, I learned that in my county alone over the period of a year, eighteen schoolchildren had been slain by guns while attending classes, more than the total number of gun killings in the entire nation of Australia. Bob Herbert in his previously cited *New York Times* article reported: 'An average of fourteen children and teenagers are killed with guns each day. Firearms kill more people between the ages of fifteen and twenty-four than all other causes combined.'

It seems to me that this particular form of firearm death could be easily controlled because, after all, most children could be easily protected in their school buildings. But an experienced teacher corrected me: 'Not so. Hoodlums sneak into the school to execute revenge murders. Since a shocking number of school-children bring hidden guns to class with them, the deaths will continue.' As if to confirm that prediction, a few weeks after that conversation the Supreme Court reversed a law that had banned guns within a thousand yards of any school. In effect the justices said that gun owners have constitutional rights that take prece-dence over the rights of children to continue living.

I believe that guns are such an integral part of American soci-ety, so deeply ingrained in our national psyche, that we will never be able to bring them under control. The people west of the Mississippi will not allow it. We have chosen the path of Sparta, not Athens, and we may not be able to rectify that wrong decision.

A disturbing development is the proliferation, especially in the West and the South, of so-called militia units. These are paramil-itary groups of men and women with guns and uniforms who train like soldiers in the countryside, practicing against the day when they may have to defend themselves against the tyranny of the government.

Historically their roots reach far back in American history. When I was a boy in a Pennsylvania town the highlight of the year so far as public spectacles were concerned was the Fourth of July parade in which the marchers included veterans of the Civil War. In a neighboring town we had a man whose proud accom-plishment was his membership in the time-honored Philadel-phia Cavalry, which dated back to the Revolutionary War. His uniform was a dazzling affair seen to good advantage whenever the Cavalry formed the guard of honor for notables who visited Philadelphia.

There were also the men's organizations that reenacted Civil War battles wearing uniforms of the period, but the one that capped them all was the re-creation of George Washington's crossing the Delaware River on December 26 to take the British army by surprise in the Battle of Trenton. We had a man who looked a spitting image of Washington, we had the boat and the cadre of patriots who crossed the river at the exact spot where Washington did. One winter I was Colonel Knox, Washington's aide, and nearly froze in the bitter cold.

None of these military reenactments did any harm; they simply reminded us of our glorious history. But about 1960 a different element of society took over the celebrations and injected a darker agenda. Across the nation this element was able to convert many of the harmless military celebrations into celebrations of the so-called militia with its doctrine of hatred of our civil government and its plan to take control when enough militias functioned in the states, especially west of the Mississippi. They constitute a perversion of our American heritage; it is true that the colonial militia organizations such as the minutemen took up arms in defiance of their government, but the monarchical government in England was truly oppressive and the colonies could not resort to the ballot box in order to improve their lot.

The members of the militias are intensely patriotic, and they yearn to return to the good old days of family solidarity. They despise our present government, especially if it happens to be in Democratic hands; they are committed both to their beliefs that the government is secretly plotting to deprive them of their freedoms and to their intrigues against the government. While they are not openly racist, they are preponderantly white Anglo-Saxons and their ranks provide a haven for those who fear the ultimate domination of the races of color, whether the imagined enemy happens to be black, brown or yellow.

From listening to their rhetoric I judge that many of their members believe that concessions to minorities have gone too far too fast, and that ordinary white men like themselves have been penalized by affirmative action. They believe that specific advantages given the minorities should be halted and that the general trend in that direction should be reversed.

Passionately they believe they have been organized to save the nation from revolution and expect to be called to arms in the foreseeable future. In religion they are often believers in the Book of Revelation and its turgid nonsense, but they do not take sides in any debate between Catholicism and Protestantism; a goodly number of their rabid members claim to be born–again right–wing Christians.

Listening to the preachings of the self–styled leaders of the militia movement I suspect that there is a high percentage of weirdos and semipsychopaths in the ranks, but I have also found no evidence that they actually preach overt rebellion and certainly they do not equate their violent speech with treason. They passionately believe that they are striving to save the United States from itself.

But law–abiding though they claim themselves to be, the heart of their movement is the gun. The forces that keep them cohesive are the military drills, the bivouacs in the open field and the simulated defeat of an imaginary enemy defined as the government itself.

They sponsor macho values to an almost ridiculous degree, and seem inherently either to fear women or to hold them in benign contempt. They are becoming a silent force in American life; once restricted to our western states, especially those beyond the Mississippi, they have in recent years established footholds in the South and East.

Do they do much harm? Do they pose a major threat to our social and political structure? I hope not. They are a minor social aberration, which sees plots against them and their ideals in the most ordinary acts of government. One spokesman even views the move of our government to produce paper money that cannot be easily counterfeited as a plot to destroy our money system and wrest their savings from them. And all the groups preach that the government's criminal behavior in wiping out the Branch Davidian cult at Waco, Texas, was a warning of what the militiamen might expect in the future. Waco is a rallying cry of the militia movement.

In politics the militias do not choose sides, but one supposes that 90 percent of the membership votes Republican and heartily endorses recent swings toward the center or even back to the extreme right. And these are people who *will* vote when they fear their interests are threatened.

When an old friend, whom I will call Bud Kelly, from Iowa soloed down to Texas in his private plane, he brought me a new interpretation of the militia movement. He was choleric about the dictatorial behavior of the air traffic control officials who had given him a bad time when he was in his approach. His face reddening, he growled: 'No wonder people are flocking to the militia units. If I ran into one of the members right now, I'd join.'

'Wait a minute, Bud!' I protested. 'Don't talk nonsense. You're a born-again Republican businessman, one of the most confirmed conservatives I know and a sensible observer of politics and business economics. You're not the militia type.'

'You miss the point, Jim. I'm just the type that's been joining their movement, because my contacts with government are all sour. Two-bit tyrants tell me how to fly my plane. They tell me who I can hire in my office—so many of these, so many of those—and they intrude maliciously in every damned thing I want to do. I'm ready for the militia, because they talk sense.'

'Maybe so, but you aren't. Bud, you aren't the type.'

'That's the point. I am. I'm the outraged citizen who feels the pressure of government, the tyranny, if you will, and I'm getting sick of it. The militia is the only way I can strike back.'

After a long evening exploring his rage, I concluded: 'If a man like you can seriously consider volunteering for the militia, this nation is in trouble.' And he replied: 'Yes, we are. The oppression has to be stopped.'

But I hope people like Bud will come to realize that the way to stop what he calls the oppression is to work for government re- form in a responsible way.

Coincident with the growth of the militia movement, although not specifically related to it, has been the phenomenal explosion of radio talk shows. They have become today's public forum, the New England town meeting of the past. They reach into all cor- ners of the nation and are more addictive than nicotine. One would think that such public discussion would be beneficial, but instead of a legitimate airing of issues it is a macho, one-sided di- atribe almost exclusively right-wing in orientation. Many are masterminded at the microphones by those who are not afraid to indulge in a virulence not heard before over the airwaves. The violence of their discourse and their lack of civility are part and parcel of their macho posturings, and it is not uncommon to hear what can only be interpreted as veiled invitations to murder the president. Character assassination is the daily stock-in-trade; by the very nature of the format, the victim has no recourse to any form of rebuttal.

During periods when I have been temporarily incapacitated, I have listened to many hours of talk radio and have been ap- palled at the flagrant attacks on decency and the unfounded ac- cusations against our political leaders. At least 90 percent of those practicing this new art form are strong right-wing advocates. Normal discourse is impossible, and the listener is seduced into believing that the entire drift of the nation is to the extreme right with an obligation to abolish the liberal legislation of the past decades.

Talk radio has been enormously effective in branding liberals as either addlepated do-gooders or downright subversives out to destroy the republic. Since there has been no powerful rejection of this charge against the liberals, there is a strong possibility that this skewed interpretation of legitimate liberalism will become the conventional wisdom of the future. How our nation has allowed and even applauded this sudden reversal of its long traditions bewilders me. It is not healthy for our society and, if allowed to fully take root, will lead to an American version of fascism.

Perhaps an agency with adequate funding could be established to report to the general public exactly what it is that talk radio is sponsoring and how it pollutes the air in which it reigns supreme at the moment. The most offensive statements, such as the following, could be identified and rebutted.

The exhortation that the listener should shoot any government official in uniform who tries to enforce government laws in one's vicinity. This general suggestion was later refined with advice not to aim at the chest, because agents wear bulletproof vests—aim at the head.

The charge that President Clinton masterminded the murder of a political foe back in Arkansas.

The accusation that Hillary Clinton is leading a secret plot to deny medical doctors their fees and their freedoms.

The charge that a band of secretive congressmen run the government and pay heed to foreign interests rather than our own.

The accusation that 'they' are subversively gaining control of our national water supplies with the aim of determining how much food can be grown on our farms.

During the TV talk shows I viewed in my enforced idleness, I, like most of the uninitiated, was sickened by the parade of social deviates, malcontents and revolutionaries: two sisters sleeping with the same man, another man sleeping with both mother and daughter, and almost every other combination of sleeping arrangements. But I was frightened by the constant supply of hard revolutionaries like the skinheads, the white supremacists, the angry men who said they would fight to halt quota hiring for blacks, Hispanics and women, and the confused young men and women who could not identify a specific enemy but who lashed out against society in general. They displayed such an array of social dysfunction, and they were in such constant supply day after day, that I sometimes thought they represented a new nation in which I was a stranger.

What surprised me about this collection of society's avowed enemies was that no matter how preposterous their accusations against the government or traditional society, and no matter how violent the remedies they envisioned, whatever they said tended to bring enthusiastic applause from a large portion of the audience. It is possible that this viewer applause is nothing more than a cathartic release from the tedium of a humdrum life, but more likely it represents support for the insane ideas being promulgated.

After one ugly morning when skinheads vilified Jews, liberals and women to loud applause I thought: This is frightening. If a viewer is already on the border of deviate or destructive behavior he could be lured over the edge by such a constant reinforcement of his suspicions. I am convinced that these sick manifestations of despair can have dangerous repercussions. But when I voice my apprehensions to others, they tend to say that all the violent talk is harmless because it has little or no effect on the listener.

I fear such reasoning is comparable to the specious argument that children are not influenced by the onslaught of violence, mayhem and murder they see on television. If hearing a great symphony or seeing a fine play can have a positive, calming and constructive effect, watching a parade of brutality can certainly have a deleteriously negative effect. For its own self-defense, the federal government should monitor the worst of these brutal shows, but it obviously cannot because it would be accused of censorship.

One of the saddest consequences of our surrender to exaggerated macho exhibitionism has been the debasement of the American motion picture in which sheer brutality takes the place of orderly storytelling and reasonable character development. Again the roots of the violent movie reach back to our past. Almost from the first we had shoot-em-up westerns in which cowboys postured with guns, but soon the genre graduated to the enormously attractive films of John Wayne, who brought common sense and believable characters to his roles. Such films as *The Hunters*, which depicted Wayne and his sidekick tracking down the evil men who had stolen Wayne's sister when she was a child, were compelling pictures, while *Stage Coach* is universally considered a classic.

But relatively soon the genre again degenerated into pure macho exhibitionism, and sensible patrons stayed home and played videos of past masterpieces in their living rooms. To see those excellent films with first-class actors and actresses filling even minor roles can be a real treat. *Dinner at Eight* and *The Informer* are still wonderful to see, as are such past blockbusters as *Gone with the Wind* and *My Fair Lady*. We lose a wealth of great entertainment when we turn our movies over to mayhem and casual murders like the James Bond thrillers and Rambo epics. We could use in their place more movies like *The Grapes of Wrath*, which illuminate pages of our real history.

The motion picture industry must accept the fact that it can be equated with violence in sports, proliferation of handguns and vitriolic talk shows. It cannot escape its part of the blame for the ugly violence that is becoming so prevalent in America as a result of our glorification of the macho.

Recommendations

1. We must diminish the violence in college and professional sports.

2. Despite our national love affair with the gun, we must keep firearms out of our schools.

3. The FBI should be not only allowed but encouraged to infiltrate the militia groups and maintain watch on them. (I say this as a graduate of Swarthmore College, who is aware of what J. Edgar Hoover did to our college when he deemed it a hotbed of subversion.)

4. The excesses of talk radio should be muted, while preserving the First Amendment guarantees for free speech. But let us be mindful of Justice Holmes's often cited judgment: 'The most stringent protection of free speech would not protect a man in falsely shouting fire in a theater and causing a panic.'

5. The morning and afternoon talk shows should be discouraged from providing the avowed enemies of society a platform on which to parade their hideous views and gain converts while doing so.

6. In the endless struggle for the soul of our nation, let us think more of Athens than of Sparta.

Ten

Art in Society

*H*aving spent most of my life studying the arts and having devoted much of my income to their furtherance, I have acquired strong feelings about their place in a democracy. When I say 'arts' I speak of the entire spectrum of the field: from ceramics and dance in the ancient world, to the flowering of the visual arts during the Renaissance, to the wonderful world of music in the eighteenth and nineteenth centuries, to the glories of Impressionism at the close of the last century, to the explosion of new visual forms in the best work done by the New York School starting in the 1950s. I specifically include motion pictures and drama, opera and architecture.

For me, the arts have been a wonderland that I explored as if I were a perpetual ten-year-old always discovering fresh excitements. The arts have helped create a civilization of which I have been proud to be a part, and they have vastly enriched my life. I feel almost a blood relationship with all the artists in all the mediums, for I find that we face the same problems but solve them in our own ways. When young people in my writing classes, for example, ask what subjects they should study if they wish to become writers, I surprise them by replying: 'Ceramics and eurythmic dancing.' When they look surprised I explain: 'Ceramics so you can feel form evolving through your fingertips molding the moist clay, and eurythmic dancing so you can experience the flow of motion through your body. You might develop a sense of freedom that way.'

If an aspiring writer assures me that she or he received A's in English I am not impressed, because anyone ought to be able to get an A in English. But if she or he also says: 'I received an A in architecture,' I feel there might be potential in that person because I can assume the speaker has a feeling for form, which is the sense of balance that is essential for both a building and a novel to create a vibrant impression.

When I was striving to develop my own method of storytelling, I was helped enormously by an orchestra concert I heard. The featured work was Beethoven's Piano Concerto No. 4, which opens with crashing chords from the piano, as if to alert the audience that the piano is going to be very important. It then falls silent while the other instruments of the orchestra lay a solid groundwork, then it magnificently rejoins and blends with the orchestra. I told myself that evening: If Beethoven can keep the primary instrument silent for so long, I can do the same with my novels: Establish a theme but don't bring any human characters into play until many pages later. That device, which I learned through music, has served me well.

Later in life I put together a master collection of Japanese prints, especially the landscapes of Hokusai and Hiroshige, and through studying them I learned how to view outdoor nature. In time I would become well known for my faithful description and wide use of landscape in my novels. And from the brilliant canvases of the early Italian Renaissance I learned what color was and how to achieve its effects in words.

I have been well served by the arts, and have lived in close contact with orchestras and opera companies and art museums, always with rewarding results. I cannot conceive how any city can describe itself as major if it does not provide its citizens with experiences in the arts. And I believe that performing groups like dance companies and repertoire theater companies, and large establishments with fixed costs like orchestra halls and opera houses, should be supported by tax funds. I realize that in admitting this I am flying in the face of the current wisdom. Under the new government today, a powerful assault is being made on all the arts, and the targets include the individual such as a painter, the group like a dance company, the institution like an opera house, or a television station that presumes to offer cultural programming.

I find it perplexing that our new Congress seems determined to strangle the arts. The Contract with the American Family blatantly calls for the cessation of all public funds for the arts, and while Newt Gingrich's Contract with America refrains from a frontal assault, the actions of his Congress speak for him: subsidies for the arts will have to go.

I cannot understand why the proponents of the contracts seem to believe that killing off funds for the arts will strengthen family life or help to create a stronger nation. Does the cultivation of beauty–great theater, superb orchestral performances–add nothing to American life?

In 1996 the members of Congress have delighted in castigating the arts as if they and their creators exert an influence that is somehow poisonous. And some of the public is applauding. But ten years from now, when these same legislators are older and perhaps wealthier and they decide to take a vacation in Europe, what do they and their families want to see? Not the Rolls-Royce plant and not the headquarters of a great international bank in London, nor the operations of the French railway system, which is so much more effectively run than ours. No, our visitors know what makes a trip to Europe meaningful. They want to see where Charles Dickens lived, or the moors about which Thomas Hardy wrote, or Stratford-on-Avon, where William Shakespeare honed his mastery of words. They want to see where Cézanne painted or view the art treasures of the Vatican, including that immortal chapel decorated primarily by Michelangelo. They want to hear a Verdi opera at La Scala or a Wagner opus in Bayreuth or experience the majesty of Florence and the joie de vivre of Venice. They want to tour the Louvre and the Prado and the National Gallery in London.

Our American visitors to Europe are not stupid. They know what greatness is, and if they can spot it only in Europe and rarely in their own backyard, when they are abroad they are eager to pay their respects to it.

Therefore I cannot understand why our new leaders attack the arts with such venom. I sometimes feel they hate the arts more than they do child pornography, and this bespeaks an ignorance about what makes the civilization of any nation memorable. If our new masters have their way, tax support for the arts would decline to near zero, an act of folly that will elicit censorious comments from the nations with which we compete.

In most of the major nations, even including some in South and Central America, public funds are allotted to the arts. Great museums are built and publicly funded. Performing companies enjoy public support; individual artists receive help from state-administered funds. The governments understand and fulfill their obligations to take what steps they can afford to spur the arts generally. If such a symbiotic relationship exists in large parts of the world, it must be because the nations appreciate the great good that art contributes to their societies.

And one of the major contributions that art brings to a community is money. When theaters are crowded, hotels, restaurants and taxicabs prosper. When an arts festival is held, the public pours money into the area in which it is offered. When a group of fine paintings come up for auction, the evening's take might reach $60 million, much of it taxable. And a city or a district that becomes famous for the excellence of its art–like Boston for its symphony, Santa Fe for its opera, Tanglewood for its summer concerts, Assisi for the frescoes depicting the life of Saint Francis, or Florence for the richness of the art displayed at the Uffizi– collects not only substantial income from ticket sales but also tax funds from the general economy of the region. Crassly put: art means money.

I speak with a certain familiarity with this important aspect of creative activity. Some years ago, before I had even written most of my big books, an accountant calculated that the government had collected some $60 million in taxes on my works and from their subsequent lives as plays, musicals, movies and television programs. The figure did not come solely from my taxes, al- though I certainly contributed generously; it also included taxes on the salaries and the production costs and the price of admis- sion tickets to works that other artists had based upon my nov- els. And my contributions are modest compared with the national income derived from blockbuster motion pictures today.

So when I listen to our national leaders blasting the arts, and when I hear that in their plans for the future they propose to sti- fle the arts and deny them sustenance, I think: How shortsighted! They are killing a goose that lays golden eggs.

The presence of art more than pays its way, and the world's hunger for the best keeps the art world functioning. Why did thousands of people from all over the world crowd into a little town in southern France to visit a cave at Lascaux? They had come to view art–in my case, to pay profound, almost religious respect. On the walls of the dark cave prehistoric artists of 14,000 B.C. engraved or sketched or painted the world's oldest surviving art, probably created for public ritual or worship. So many tourists and art lovers elbowed their way into the cave that the French government had to ration admittance lest perspiration and moisture-laden breath destroy the art.

But I have been speaking only of the utilitarian value of the arts. More vital, I think, are the spiritual values that art brings to a nation. How inestimable in value to the French people has been their magnificent "La Marseillaise"! What tremendous power it has to inspirit an entire nation! How the world responds to the seraphic beauty of the choral movement of Beethoven's Ninth Symphony! How gently Fra Angelico's fresco of *The Annunciation* can affect the mind and one's spiritual impulses! With what awe we stare at Michelangelo's Sistine paintings! And how like the voice of heaven do the chords of Palestrina's *Missa Papae Marcelli* echo in our minds!

I have used exclamation marks in the above paragraph because such experiences reach one's very soul. I hope that there are many among my readers who can recall those moments of revelation when their levels of understanding were altered. Perhaps it was a performance of *Death of a Salesman* or *A Streetcar Named Desire* or even the movie *E.T.* The arts can truly lift us out of ourselves in a way that nothing else can.

I hope I have made it clear that I enthusiastically support projects that pump tax dollars into the art institutions like orchestras, ballet companies, grand operas and museums. To invest in such activity is to gamble intelligently on the future of the community. But now we come to a more debatable aspect of the problem: Should tax dollars be allocated to individual artists so that they can pursue their vocation? Should committees be given the responsibility for identifying which individual artists are to receive a governmental stipend?

A large portion of the harsh anti-art agitation of recent years in America has stemmed from grants to individuals whose work or behavior has turned sour, and from the blatant exhibitionism of publicity-seeking undisciplined artists whose extravagant public performances have insulted and outraged the general public, bringing opprobrium not only on themselves but also on the arts and artists generally.

An exhibition of the work of one artist, the gifted photographer Robert Mapplethorpe, was mounted with primarily fine photographs of standard subject matter. But mixed in with such shots was a series of what the public considered offensively explicit erotic scenes, particularly those depicting naked males in various suggestive poses.

Since government funds had helped support the exhibition, there was a public outcry. Two different major museums handled the exhibit in similar ways, but with vastly different results. At the distinguished Philadelphia Institute of Contemporary Art the show was arranged for the public with full fanfare, but in the spaces open to the general public only the noncontroversial photographs were shown. Far off to one side in a corner not easily approached by the public but available to it if visitors asked to see them, were the sexually explicit photos.

There was not a word of protest. The artistic integrity of the museum was protected, censorship was not practiced and the public could see some fine photographic work. I thought at the time: Precisely the strategy followed for the last two hundred years with the erotic murals at Pompeii–they've been preserved, but they're not thrown in the public's face.

How different from what happened in Cincinnati. Despite the care taken by that city's Contemporary Arts Center to isolate five images of homosexual acts, to put up warnings about the subject matter of the photos and to prohibit children from viewing any of the works, the result was a loud outcry, strong protests, an indictment of the museum and its director on obscenity charges, and a scandalous court case. A hasty marshaling of experts from the artistic and cultural community–not only in Cincinnati–rushed to defend the director, but the city was seen nationwide as a censorious philistine town and received a black eye it did not merit. I am at a complete loss as to why the public reception in Cincinnati was so different from that in Philadelphia, since both museums handled the delicate situation in equally sensitive and intelligent ways.

I personally spoke out in defense of Mapplethorpe and decried the censorship that had motivated the trial surrounding his work, for I had taken an oath that all my public life I would defend the free-speech article of the Bill of Rights. I have done so whenever books like Mark Twain's *Huckleberry Finn* have been attacked by self-appointed censors. I take my direction from Justice Hugo Black of our Supreme Court, who preached repeatedly in his decisions that the First Amendment meant what it said: 'Congress shall make no law abridging the freedom of speech, or of the press.'

So I would defend Mapplethorpe's photographs, all of them, and the work of the young iconoclast Andres Serrano, who placed a crucifix in a jar of urine and called it a work of art. As a former navy officer, I salute the flag and, after a long absence from home, choke up when I see it flying in the breeze, but I would also defend the flag burner on the grounds that even his reprehensible action is an expression of free speech.

I have abided by that promise to myself to combat censorship, but when faced by horrendous wrongs in our society I have found that I simply cannot defend child pornographers or lyricists who compose vile songs in which they advocate the killing or debasement of women or of policemen. Those malefactors have surrendered any claim to my support. And, to return to Mapplethorpe, while I would place his art under the protection of the

Bill of Rights, I could not defend the financing and display of his art with public funds. Some of his art, and I recognize that it *is* art, is seemingly intended to infuriate the sensibilities of commonly accepted morality. And it should also be recognized that it will not accomplish the purpose of the expenditure of tax dollars on art as a spiritual, financial and social asset of the community.

That still leaves the problem: Should tax dollars be allocated by committee vote to individual artists? This is a painful question for me to address, because my writing career has been unbelievably fortunate, and it ill behooves me to speak out against much-needed grants to deserving individual artists even though I myself did not require such aid. My decision runs much deeper than the channels of personal need, however, and I am against the grant system to individuals for many reasons. It is almost impossible to administer it justly. Despite every precaution it degenerates into a you–scratch–my–back–I'll–scratch–yours operation. Men and women of real talent are rarely identified and thrown forward by the system, and daring artists in any field are infrequently awarded grants. Most significant, through the long reach of history the productive artist has most often come from that group of aspirants who work by themselves in such quarters as they can afford and in the lively competition of the market-place.

Because such counsel, coming from me with all the advantages I have enjoyed, must sound callous and lacking in compassion, I can only say that I have always been aware of the vulnerability of unestablished writers and, because I have been excessively rewarded, have given most of the earnings of my writing to help those in the profession who were less fortunate than I was.

I realize that there seems to be a contradiction between the two parts of my advice about financing the arts: Funds for groups but not for individuals. My reasoning is this: The performance of a play, an opera or an orchestra concert requires so many different participants and so much infrastructure, such as halls, dressing rooms and support staff like stagehands, that outside financial aid is almost obligatory, while the individual artists can work and perform alone. I believe this is a real distinction.

I feel similarly about the acquisition programs of art museums. It would be unfair for a museum's board of directors to expect a curator using tax funds to purchase avant-garde art, even though often that might be the only kind worth collecting. Think, however, how the curator in the 1910 period would have been treated by the public if he had recommended the purchase of a portrait of a two-headed woman by an unknown Spanish painter named Picasso. Or should a curator using public funds be expected in the 1950s to buy for his local museum one of Willem de Kooning's startling distorted portraits of women? Much better, I think, to encourage private individuals to do the collecting with their own money and in time turn the results over to some responsible museum as a gift to the community.

I was fascinated some years ago when the curators of the Philadelphia Museum of Art went back in history for nearly a hundred years and gathered together from many sources canvases that had been shown in the yearly exhibitions in that city. The display was dazzling, and had the museum staff bought only one painting a year, exercising superior judgment, the city would now have a collection of a hundred master paintings. But very few of them could have been purchased in years like 1869, 1897 and 1922, when expenditure of public funds for art of an unconventional kind would have been vociferously criticized. Philadelphia was also not yet ready for the avant-garde, and so did not purchase what could have been a master collection. However, even though the officials of the museum had not dared to buy the best, a scattering of private citizens were more venturesome.

They acquired some stunning canvases and in time turned them over to the museum.

To summarize my advice to the government: Support the art groups with tax dollars, stop the wasteful and unproductive system of grants to individuals, and encourage private citizens to purchase art and pass it along to public institutions. But whatever you do, encourage the public to support art programs in the schools, facilitate art festivals in the countryside, and establish the image of a nation that loves and respects the arts, for that is one of the hallmarks of a first-rate civilization.

Despite the present round of vicious attacks on the arts, I am reassured by the fact that in certain aspects we still have superb and almost supreme manifestations of our support for the more exalted forms of culture. In Boston, Philadelphia and New York we have world-class orchestras, with Chicago and Cleveland not far behind. In the Metropolitan in New York and the National Gallery in Washington we have collections of paintings that summarize the best in Western accomplishment, while the Modern in New York and the Getty in California are gems in their fields. The Metropolitan Opera in New York sets the standard for the world, as good in its performances as La Scala in Milan, and first-rate companies perform operas in many American cities. Broadway still vies with London for leadership in world theater, and the proliferation of theater groups throughout the nation is a tribute to our enlightened citizenry. The arts are alive, and it is a responsibility of our government to see that they remain so. It would be economically stupid to deny them tax support when they not only contribute so much to us spiritually but also stimulate the economy and pay back in taxes such a large proportion of what they receive.

To exemplify what can be accomplished by groups of private citizens, even without the infusion of great amounts of tax dollars, I want to identify and praise four small museums, tucked away in odd corners of our nation, which represent local activity at its best. If you and your family are traveling in the West it would be worth a detour to go to the northwest corner of Wyoming, where the small town of Cody nestles among the hills and houses the Buffalo Bill Museum. Started in the town in which members of Buffalo Bill Cody's descendants still live, it was little more than a minor tourist stop until a group of enthusiasts from all parts of the United States took an interest in it, and with their financial and administrative support quickly transformed it into a small but magnificent museum near the eastern entrance to Yellowstone National Park. It now consists of four separate museums: one honors Buffalo Bill and his flamboyant life; another houses probably the premier collection of Western art in the world, the Remingtons and the Russells and the best examples of so-called cowboy art; the third, a big, striking museum honoring the American Indian, has become the jewel of the lot, a surprise to the casual visitor who might not have been aware of the richness of Native American art; and the final museum has been contributed by the Winchester people, who have placed here their impressive collection of American firearms, including rare examples of their own product, 'the gun that won the West.'

I have for many years been affiliated with the Cody and have marveled at its transformation into something fresh and new and better. It is a magnificent tribute to the people, especially those living in distant New York who have supported it.

In the west Texas cow town of Lubbock, Texas Tech University has created a museum of the Western rancher. On one of its fields imaginative professors of the institution have brought in bulldozers to erect substantial berms (artificial low walls constructed by bulldozing loose earth into position) to break the flat prairie into a score of nests each about the size of a tennis court or larger.

Into these earthen receptacles people of the university moved–
one building to each bermed holding area–a collection of the
actual houses, barns and workshops in which the ranchers of
the area had lived. Into one big bermed nest they moved an
entire barn, and into the smaller area across the way they imported a ranch house from seventy miles out in the country.

In time they covered a huge portion of their prairie land, with
the pleasing result that the university now has an imposing outdoor museum of western ranch life. This is an outdoor museum
worth seeing.

Equally imaginative are two small museums in the Philadelphia area, because they show what almost any community with
imagination can achieve. Southwest of the major city in the pic-
turesque village of Chadds Ford, near the Delaware state line,
members of the Wyeth family of artists and their supporters have
transformed a nineteenth–century gristmill into a lovely museum
featuring the works of the family. It is a handsome place, well run
and a delight to visit.

At about the same distance from central Philadelphia but to
the northeast in the onetime village of Doylestown, Pennsylvania, a group of energetic young men convinced the political
leaders of the area that the government should give them the
remnants of a handsome old jail built of native stone in the 1860s.
They converted this into a museum honoring the Pennsylvania
impressionists, that surprising group of some dozen fine artists
who settled in Bucks County at the turn of the century and made
the area an art center for the times. Later, a score of famous writers came into the area–Sid Perelman, Oscar Hammerstein, Pearl
Buck, the Broadway masters George S. Kaufman and Moss Hart,
Dorothy Parker and others–so the museum contains not only
paintings by the early artists but also memorial tributes to the
writers. The unused jail has been transformed into an art museum

that has become the pride of the community and a vital center for the education of children. This kind of imaginative use of our heritage is available to almost any community in the United States.

I believe that the four museums I've listed have been constructed without relying excessively on tax funds, but if the time comes when such assistance is required, funds should be made available; centers of interest like these are invaluable. They illuminate and inspire entire populations and make themselves a functioning part of a community.

There remains the perplexing question of why in recent years there has suddenly been a groundswell of opposition to the arts. For an answer one must look at the composition and behavior of the new political leaders who have suddenly found themselves responsible for dealing with this problem of the arts in an essentially macho society. Their commander, House Speaker Newt Gingrich, is himself an intellectual, a reader of books, a college professor and the author of a novel, with other books contracted for, but he and most of his followers appear to me to be viscerally anti-intellectual and ill disposed to provide funding for the arts. The Contract with the American Family declares open warfare on the arts in a spirit of crude anti-intellectualism. Its authors would have us believe that modern society can be governed only by people of a stolid, unimaginative middle class, but a democracy in particular requires public servants with a vibrant outlook to keep it functioning and healthy and in touch with modern developments.

The unfortunate cases I've referred to earlier–the erotic Mapplethorpe photographs of nude males, the crucifix in urine, the desecration of the flag–have handed the critics powerful clubs with which to attack the arts, the artists and especially the public funding. Their virulence is such that I am reminded of the quotation attributed to Hermann Göring: 'When I hear somebody say the word *culture,* I reach for my revolver.' Such a remark is particularly reprehensible coming from a man who assembled a priceless collection of paintings stolen from the art museums in the European cities conquered by the Nazis.

I am confused when officials from the extreme right propose in *their* contract, which they call the Contract with the American Family, the abolishment of all funds for intellectual programs and especially the gutting of the PBS broadcasts that have been so helpful in educating our preschool children. They seem ignorant of the fact that the arts—along with professional sports—have been one of the ladders by which gifted young people in the inner cities can climb out of their ghettos. How does the strangulation of such programs strengthen family life?

The arts face a threefold crisis: First, the new political leaders seem to both despise and fear the arts, and they are trying to persuade the general public to agree with them; second, the new managers are determined to abolish all grants of tax money for the arts; and, third, some of the manifestations of our current arts, like gangsta rap, are so patently offensive that Robert Dole, the former Senate majority leader and the 1996 Republican presidential candidate, gained wide support when he inveighed publicly against specific companies for their contamination of American popular culture. I agree with him on his condemnation of lyrics that debase women and encourage young punks to shoot police officers. I have stated earlier that I would not defend this sort of speech under the First Amendment. Dole's accusations formed a test case for me as to whether I really meant what I said. I did, and I support him in his attack on that hideous music.

Where the widespread attack on the arts will end I cannot guess. Occasional excesses render them vulnerable, and tax funds are visibly wasted in a handful of the grants, but it is irrational to condemn an entire segment of our society, and one that contributes so much. To do so depicts us as boorish oafs to the foreign nations with which we must do business, and we broadcast to the world the word that in America Billy–Bob Bubba has replaced Ralph Waldo Emerson.

I hope a truce can be devised between those attacking the arts and those defending them, for to continue the enmity as it exists at present is worse than counterproductive.

Recommendations

1. Before agreeing to eviscerate the arts, Congress should make a careful analysis of how much the arts contribute to American life in economics, in adding to the good reputation of our country, in providing entertainment and creative use of recreation and, most important of all, to the spiritual well–being of our society.

2. If the study shows that the contributions of art in these fields is positive, as I believe it will, widespread attacks on them will probably cease.

3. Tax funds that have been cut or threatened should be re-studied. Art is unquestionably a sound investment for a nation, a city, a family or an individual.

4. Support with tax funds those performance units that require large numbers of participants, such as symphony orchestras, dance ensembles and small regional theaters.

5. Halt the funding of individuals selected by committee.

6. Defend the freedom of speech promised in the First Amendment, but differentiate between avant–garde groundbreaking art and exhortations to go and kill a cop.

7. Our general society must encourage the custodians of our museums, libraries and universities to keep informed about new trends and the avant–garde and not to be mired in the tried and true. But curators supported by public tax money should not purchase what the public might deem too extreme. Such art should be purchased by individual citizens and, in time, turned over to the museums.

8. The word *art* represents the total human experience in its search for beauty, clarification and instruction. It encompasses music, painting, poetry, novels, ceramics, dance, motion pictures, architecture and even television. The easiest art object for the general public to create is a well–planned city or town.

Eleven

The
Young
Colonels

*T*hrough the ebb and flow of contemporary history, I have observed, sometimes at close hand, the overthrow of one or another democratic society by a military dictatorship. Such a takeover has often been termed 'a revolt of the generals,' but this label is often erroneous. Many times the rebellions are led not by venerable commanding generals but by young colonels who have convinced themselves that their civilian–led society is corrupt and that their generals are afraid to take corrective action. The younger men, fearing that time is being lost, take radical action, close down the duly elected governing agencies, such as the parliaments, and sometimes even oust the indecisive generals.

This phenomenon has become so frequent in recent years that one can anticipate the probable steps the young colonels will take. But first it will be helpful to look back in history and see how often in crucial periods the young men of a nation have grabbed the reins of government. I think one must characterize Napoleon's takeover of the French government in 1799 in that light, and his subsequent rise to the dictatorship of France was the logical consequence of his coup d'état. Of course he was not technically a colonel when this happened–he had already been named general in 1793 at the age of twenty–four–but he was for many years known as 'the little corporal.'

Adolf Hitler also exhibited as a corporal most of the qualities of an aggressive young colonel in that he successfully led a revolution against the civilian agencies of government and then skillfully replaced the military leaders of the nation by manipulating affairs so that they were neutralized. In a series of brilliant moves, he captured the leadership of the army and acquired enough personal power to lead his nation on its mad rampage of opposition to Jews, Gypsies, homosexuals, liberals and ultimately all of Europe and Russia. He remains the archetype of what a young colonel is capable of when allowed to run rampant in a society. The final Allied bombing of Berlin and Dresden and the fall of a once great nation should forever be a warning to all countries that power surrendered to a dictatorship can only lead to evil and ultimately to the destruction of the state.

In recent times the rebellion in the black republic of Liberia was led by young officers, and in Algeria it was again the young military men who led the prolonged but ultimately futile struggle for the establishment of a rigid Muslim state. In Haiti, under "Baby Doc" Duvalier, it was the young officers who maintained the dictatorship, and in numerous South and Central American countries it has been the young colonels who have led the way.

Since the takeover of so many governments followed more or less the same pattern, it is possible to codify the common principles governing the behavior of the young rebels:

They have all been motivated by a fierce patriotism and a determination to protect their nation, but it is noteworthy that Napoleon was not a native-born Frenchman nor Hitler a German.

The idealistic young colonels all want to guide their nations back to some dream period when a moral type of life prevailed. They are infected with nostalgia and deluded as to what the 'purer' former life had been. But they persist in their dedication to the past and are determined to turn back the clock till the days of supposed glory are recovered.

They are instinctively afraid of intellectually superior people and take savage steps to control or even eliminate them.

They cannot trust artists and take harsh steps to discipline them or forbid them to practice their skills.

They loudly proclaim that they support and defend family values–whatever the young men consider them to be–but their actions are almost always destructive of the family.

For reasons I do not understand but whose bad results I have often witnessed, they seem to be afraid of women, especially young women at the height of their sexual allure, and they pass drastic edicts aimed at bringing them under control. Women do not prosper in the revolutions; the Nazi prescription for a woman's life was '*Kirche, Kinder, Küche*' (church, children, kitchen).

In lands governed by Muslim law the young colonels enact the most repressive rules, severely enforcing old and outmoded religious laws against women that previous and more liberal governments had relaxed. In many countries the women must return to the veil that covers their faces in public; others have been chastised for driving their own automobiles; and in the worst instances, some women have been executed for not adhering to the new rules.

Regarding religion, the young colonels are apt to be ambivalent. They say they subscribe to the most conservative forms of worship but they do not treat organized religion kindly. They demand that it serve as an agency of the new state, not as a protector of human values.

Sad to say, the revolutions usually deteriorate in purpose so that thousands and even millions of lives are lost. The awful example of this in recent times was the murder of thousands of intellectuals and liberals by the young colonels of the Argentine takeover. The killings in Algeria have also been persistent and gruesome.

Because of their association with civil leaders, most of whom happen to be wealthy, the colonels seem almost to worship persons with large fortunes, and the new laws they initiate invariably favor the wealthy and penalize the poor. Even in the few cases in which the colonels seriously intend to better the conditions of the poor, they wind up favoring the rich.

Human nature being what it is, I would expect such revolts by young colonels to occur in many nations through the foreseeable future, and I suppose that most of them will follow the traditions of the past. Young conservatives will always want to lead their nations back to the past days of a simpler life, a more rigidly patriotic citizenry and a sense of discipline as defined by themselves. I view the 1994 congressional election as a sweeping victory of the young colonels, American style.

A major and vitally important difference between the Republican young colonels and their European and South American counterparts is, of course, that the victorious Republicans have been legally elected to their present positions of power. Nevertheless, they have been leading a revolution. They are an American phenomenon, brash young neophytes eager to throw their weight around despite their lack of political experience. They have sent an overwhelming message that they are dissatisfied with American political life as it is being conducted. These young white males are fearful that the dictates of affirmative action are giving minorities and women an advantage over them, and they want to reverse all aspects of special legislation protecting the employment of these groups. And among the public there is a general dissatisfaction with liberals, regardless of what the liberals propose. The message of antigovernment fury was so strong and so decisive in the 1994 elections that no one could miss its significance.

The young Republicans leaped into the fray with breathtaking speed, completing in their first six months in power what a more conservative and thoughtful legislative body would have required a year and a half to enact. The victorious young colonels quickly presented and passed in the House of Representatives what they termed a Contract with America, and the nation had to acknowledge that from now on things were going to be different. The social revolution that Franklin Delano Roosevelt engineered in 1932 and that Lyndon Johnson extended in the 1960s was largely to be scuttled with the major result that citizens at the lower end of the economic hierarchy would be deprived of many of their aid programs while those at the upper end would watch their fortunes grow.

Even though some of the provisions of the Contract with America passed by the House of Representatives have already been stalled in the Senate or vetoed by the president with little chance of acquiring a two-thirds override of the presidential veto, it is worthwhile to discuss the provisions here. The Contract represents a philosophy–a sometimes dangerous, self-serving philosophy–held by a large number of our citizens and congressmen. Even those provisions that have already been rejected could possibly be resurrected if the Republican Party increases the size of its majorities in Congress or if the Republicans gain possession of the Oval Office.

The contract, drafted under the supervision of Congressman Newt Gingrich, is divided into two parts. The first contains recommendations that can be imposed upon Congress without the passage of an act or the signature of the president. Some of these are housekeeping measures that everyone applauds, such as requiring Congress as a body and congressmen individually to obey all the laws that apply to the rest of the nation. Who could object to that? Other proposals curtail the cumbersome committee system. I and probably many other Americans were pleased to see these rules put in effect during the early days of the Republican revolution. But two other rules these young colonels tried to impose without formal passage of a bill gave me trouble. They advocated a three-fifths majority vote before any tax could be increased, and they wanted to discipline our budgetary process by zero baseline budgeting requiring justification each year, without factoring in inflation. Neither of these proposals has become law yet; both are flagrant attempts to curtail taxation and balance the budget, not so much for their intrinsic value but rather to protect the wealthy against taxation and ensure they can retain ever larger percentages of their growing fortunes.

The real body of the contract, the second half, outlines specific proposals, called Acts, that require approval by both houses of Congress and signature by the president. Again there are elements in the contract that a majority of the voters could probably endorse. The ones I have supported or could support if they were well drawn are the Fiscal Responsibility Act, which included giving the president line-item veto power; the Family Reinforcement Act, designed to strengthen family ties; and the National Security Restoration Act, giving the United States control of U.S. troops when serving under United Nations commanders. Unfortunately this last proposal includes a recommendation that we restore the 'essential' parts of our national security funding 'to strengthen our national defense and maintain our credibility around the world.' This is a euphemism for 'unlimited spending on the military to be paid for by termination of social services to the public.' Extreme caution should be exercised to avoid that unwise choice.

On a more positive note, the president has now been given the power to veto ridiculous or improper line items in a larger budget bill. Most modern presidents, Democrat and Republican alike, have appealed to Congress for this line-item veto power, because such a power enables them to kill egregious pork-barrel inserts in otherwise solid bills and save huge sums of tax dollars.

To strengthen family ties the Family Reinforcement Act in-cludes three proposals: in a divorce, enforce court orders handed down for the support of the children involved; offer tax incen-tives to any family that will adopt an abandoned child; and strengthen laws against child pornography. I would work to help pass each of those suggestions if they are brought before Con-gress again, but at this draft the tax credit for adoption and the legislation to collect child support payments have been vetoed as part of the balanced budget and welfare vetoes.

Our congressional young colonels very sensibly–considering the pusillanimous behavior of international bodies–want no United States troops to be placed under the control of United Nations commanders. I approve, but must point out that during the war in the Pacific I watched as British, Australian and New Zealand troops fought side by side with us, often with heroic re-sults, so I know it can be done. But I would not want our troops to be assigned as subsidiaries to a United Nations force unless we volunteer to place them under some acknowledged out-standing foreign commander of the caliber of Montgomery in the African desert, Zhukov in the rout of the Germans in Russia or the brilliant British air commanders who fought off Göring's Luftwaffe.

The young Republicans also propose a brief and attractive Common Sense Legal Reform Act, which involves 'reasonable limits on punitive damages and reform of product liability laws to stem the endless tide of litigation.' I was assured that the final act would also end the infamous 'deep-pockets rule.' It works like this: A product, clearly defective, has caused a damaging acci-dent, and the question becomes 'Who was guilty of this malfea-sance?' The trail of responsibility is easily determined from past records. 'A' manufactured the item, but he has no money to pay damages. 'B' was a retailer who sold the item, and he has deep pockets–he is rich. 'C' was the installer and did a poor job, but he is broke. 'D' inherited the item in a deal many years after 'A' made it, and so the entire burden of the case is thrown on 'B' and he must pay, primarily because he can afford to.

I had a friend who was held culpable twenty–five years after he sold a piece of equipment to later dealers. He had the deep pockets; they did not, so he had to pay. That crazy practice ought to be abolished.

When a lawyer friend read the conclusions reported above, he cautioned: 'Personally, while I agree that many punitive damage awards have been ridiculous, I find this part of the contract little more than a protection of that twenty percent of the wealthy who own eighty percent of the country. It restricts the bottom eighty percent when they have been hurt in some way by the malfeasance of the top twenty percent.'

I do not like the recommendation that we pass 'Loser pays' laws because, although it would make a litigant think twice before initiating a frivolous lawsuit, it would also make it almost impossible for a person with only moderate means to sue for damages to which he or she may be entitled.

About several of the remaining acts in this second part of the contract I have serious doubts, and even considerable fear that wrong actions are being proposed. I do not like the Taking Back Our Streets Act, for it calls for a drastic cut in funds for the prevention of crime, for a comparable increase in money for the construction of ever more jails, and for more death penalties. Those are regressive steps; the emphasis of funding should be on prevention rather than on punishment. We already have more jails than a democracy should have, and it has been proved that the death penalty accomplishes little except the removal from the streets of a specific criminal–the influence on others appears to be minimal.

The proposed Personal Responsibility Act is so draconian in its probable effect on the poor and especially on poor women with children that I find it completely outside the mainstream of American history in this century. I beg the brash young colonels to restudy this proposal and awaken themselves to the ugliness of its directives, which include: (1) Discourage pregnancy and illegitimacy by stopping welfare to minor mothers. How is the girl of fourteen going to support herself and her child? (2) Deny increased funds to the Aid to Families with Dependent Children for women who have additional children while on welfare. (3) Cut spending for all welfare programs. And (4) enact a tough two-years-and-off-the-welfare-rolls provision with stiff work requirements to promote individual responsibility; any such provision is blind to the realities of American life. In thousands of instances there are no jobs, and the deficiency is going to grow. It is folly beyond imagination to believe that a mother with no husband but two small children can 'go out and find a job.' Only one in five hundred will be able to swing this miracle, but she will be paraded on the evening news as proof that it can be done. The president has vetoed the welfare reform bill sent to him, and I pray that the two houses of Congress will reject any similar proposals in the future and instead tackle the heartbreaking problem that I identified earlier: how to create some kind of employment for citizens trapped in the bottom levels of our society.

The proposal for congressional term limits in the Citizen Legislature Act finds me perplexed, and a personal note will explain why. I ran–and usually lost–for office five times, including a backbreaking campaign for Congress in 1962, and when I wasn't running I worked for my party locally, statewide and nationally. From this experience I developed such a powerful addiction to politics that until my eighties I was involved with one government job or another. I am one of the few people you will meet who ever actually voted for the president of the United States; in 1968, when Richard Nixon defeated Hubert Humphrey, I chanced to be the presiding officer of the Pennsylvania Electoral College and on a sad, wintry day I cast my vote and the twenty-nine votes of Pennsylvania for Humphrey.

So politics is in my blood, and in beating the campaign trails I met far more good men and women, Republican and Democrat alike, than bad. And out of some fifteen rough-and-tumble campaigns I developed several generalizations. The work of an election is performed by no more than a comparative handful of devoted men and women. At election time millions of voters support one party or another, but it is misleading to claim they are all members of the party; they are really temporary supporters of it. The active membership of the party as an ongoing force in our national life is probably not over sixty or seventy thousand for either party. The decisions are made by this inner core; more important, the hard work of an election is also done by them, and I am immensely appreciative of the contributions these faithful workers make. I am partial to politicians and would appreciate being considered one.

I therefore cannot be supportive of any act that limits terms served in Congress, and I am gratified that both houses of Congress have failed to pass the necessary legislation to institute a constitutional amendment for such term limits. We need the guiding hand of the time-tested politician, and not long ago I was pleased when the Supreme Court decided that the individual states could not restrict the number of terms a man or woman could represent them in Congress. Limitation could be authorized only by an amendment to the Constitution. If a move is made in that direction I hope it will be soundly defeated. Congress needs battle-tested veterans.

Even among the provisions of the proposed acts that I in general applaud, I nevertheless find several clauses that trouble me. In the Fiscal Responsibility Act, I am fearful of the recommendation that Congress must 'live under the same budget constraints as families and businesses.' I find this to be a silly, crowd–pleasing bit of sophistry. I do not fear a reasonable amount of national debt, because being unafraid to gamble on the future is one of the traits of nations that rise to greatness. I would deplore seeing us, in the next dozen years, retrogress to a position in which there is no national debt, because to achieve this we would be forced to discard many functions that a nation should perform and, in so doing, deprive our citizens of services they have a right to expect. At this moment I am sitting in my office three or four blocks from a handsome, well–stocked city library. I am more fortunate than those in other areas where, because of budget cutbacks at all levels of government, the library doors are shut and the books do not circulate. I feel a wound in my heart each time I think of what the people have lost. Why in the world does a society exist except to provide libraries and hospitals and schools and parks and playing fields for its citizens? And it can safely go into reasonable debt to pay for them.

To make my position clear, if I were somehow in charge of our nation, as soon as the proposed new laws diminished our public debt to zero, I would immediately borrow a hundred billion dollars to spend on our national infrastructure: repaved highways, rebuilt bridges, improved airstrips, state–of–the–art aviation guidance systems, new schools, enhanced transportation for the inner cities and all the other improvements we need to keep our country thriving. Nations on the upward climb are not afraid to go into debt to provide services; it is the nation that is sliding downward that insists on a perfectly balanced budget.

In the otherwise fine Family Reinforcement Act, with its proposals regarding adoption and opposition to child pornography,
occurs the frightening clause 'strengthening rights of parents in
their children's education.' This is code-speak for the move to
issue tax-supported vouchers to families who wish to send their
children to private schools, especially parochial ones. Any such
move should be defeated, because one of the glories of American
life has been our system of free public schools. Any move that
weakens them, such as taking away substantial funds for their
upkeep, will prove damaging to the nation. I said earlier that if I
had children of school age I would probably send them to some
superior private school and pay for their education myself. I
would certainly not want to burden the taxpayers of our community to gain an advantage for my offspring.

I find it difficult to understand the venom with which many of
the young colonels view our nationally administered free-lunch
program for schoolchildren and our distribution of food certifi-
cates to the impoverished elderly. Some critics who seek to min-
imize the programs or cancel them altogether grow livid as they
rant about the waste, the socialism and the misguided humani-
tarianism in the programs, but as I remember the genesis of the
free-food operations that have been so helpful to so many, they
came into being largely because Midwestern farmers wanted a
device whereby they could dispose of their surplus crops at a
profit. Dairy farmers quickly saw that it could also be used to get
rid of their unwanted surpluses, and others jumped on the band-
wagon. It was an example of how, frequently, a move motivated
by the crassest self-interest can be massaged until it produces an
absolute good.

Fortunately, these proposals are not included in the Contract
with America. Our food programs are one of the admirable functions of our national government and I do not want to see them

turned over to the states. I cannot trust state legislatures to spend wisely or even honestly whatever funds Congress might divert to them for health programs for our senior citizens and our children.

So if we choose wisely from the many suggestions of the Contract with America, much good could be achieved, but if others of the proposals are ever passed a great deal of harm would result. As the debate began regarding the contract, the extreme right wing of the Republican Party, the religious conservatives, leaped before the television cameras to announce their own Contract with the American Family. Several of its proposals would gain approval from most citizens: elimination of current laws that place extra tax burdens on couples who marry, restriction of child pornography and a proposal to punish criminals rather than their victims.

This second contract, with the American family, has other recommendations that might gain wide acceptance, such as the right to have religious displays 'in noncompulsory settings such as courthouse lawns, high school graduation ceremonies and sports events' and the outlawing of late-term abortions.

But the hard core of the philosophy underlying both contracts is contained in the young colonels' specific legislative recommendations to diminish or eliminate budgets for social purposes like education and child care, services to women and children, and money for cultural activities such as the National Endowment for the Arts and the Humanities and public broadcasting.

I find the overall spirit of these two contracts mean, vengeful and contrary to the two-centuries-old drive for social justice in America. If the provisions are rigorously enforced, the result will be an ugly society of which I would not be proud to be a part.

I am particularly depressed to find our young colonels imitating the behavior of similar young revolutionaries I've followed in the past. Like their predecessors in one country after another, these young men seem to have a visceral fear of women and a distrust that they manifest in harshly repressive laws against women, girls and babies. If all their laws against women were enacted, life in the United States could be hell for women and for many children.

Even though the contracts do not recommend openly that affirmative action be repealed or that justifiable quotas be abolished, I have heard spokesmen for the contracts assure listeners that 'sanity would be restored in those fields,' a euphemism for 'they will be abolished.' Curtailment of affirmative action would be a major move in the wrong direction, and the fact that the Supreme Court has recently outlawed college scholarships intended only for African Americans is a warning of the dangers that lie ahead. If I sound monomaniacal on this and similar problems regarding race, I am. My wife spent her life fighting racial injustice and I try to advance her agenda. When the president of my college suffered a heart attack and died following a racial confrontation on his very liberal campus, that very night I sent the school the royalties from one of my books, to be spent on pacifying the campus through the granting of some of the demands of the black students. I feel just as strongly today. There have been grave injustices in American life and they should be rectified.

I would hope that Congress and the American voter would be intelligent enough to pass the constructive parts of the two contracts while rejecting the destructive. Some of them *have* been rejected, but usually for reasons of political necessity rather than by any rejection on the part of the young colonels of the underlying philosophies. Sensible people should encourage Congress to discriminate between the acceptable and the unacceptable in the remaining acts, which, if blindly accepted by Congress without fine-tuning in favor of a just and compassionate society, I fear will create a government that we will soon thereafter have to cleanse until it conforms more closely to the great traditions of our nation.

I am convinced that we are a people committed to justice, to the care of the less fortunate, to a breeze of freedom that flows over all our actions, and to the national characteristics of hopefulness and a willingness to take considerable risks in the present in order to safeguard our security in the future.

The new breed in Congress today exhibit an intense anti-art bias. Both the specific recommendations and the spirit in which the Contract with the American Family proposes them in the field of the arts bespeak a brutality and a know-nothingness ill suited to a democracy. There is ample evidence that the provision discontinuing all funds allocated to the Corporation for Public Broadcasting stems from the personal vendetta of the Republican leaders who feel–erroneously, I believe–that Public Broadcasting Service broadcasts are unfair to conservatives but partial to liberals. These men who would apparently like to transform the United States into today's Sparta seem determined to kill off any free expression of the arts in American life by taking away all government-financed support. Their suggestion that the funds thus lost can be made up by contributions from private individuals flies against the experience of all the major European and world capitals, which fund their arts from the government coffers much more generously than we ever have. To take away the meager government funds we now provide would be disastrous and a signal that we intend becoming a nation of boors.

The deplorably and dangerously pervasive character of the two Contracts is that they favor the rich to the detriment of the poor, the already fortunate rather than the aspiring, and the Christian conservative as opposed to the Jewish/Muslim/Native American freethinker. Indeed, the second contract, the Contract with the American Family, is the official voice of the Christian Coalition, the extreme right wing of the Christian faiths and of the new Republican Party. Do we really want to invite these reactionaries to dictate what the moral values of our society shall be? Looking at the day-to-day programs of these very conservative bodies–the agenda they are reluctant to reveal in their formal contract–I am frightened, for I have observed that when men and women of such mean spirit start to dictate national policy, moderate men like me are sooner or later outlawed too. The fire-burning puritan preacher will, in the end, turn his blaze on me, so my personal interest in the great debate now under way is not abstract. It cuts to the heart of my being, and it imperils all other moderates.

When I charge that the two contracts, taken together, reek of meanness, I do not mean this in any trivial sense. I believe the revolution of the young colonels threatens the long–established social contract that has operated in the United States since our Constitution came into being. It is that solemn agreement forged by the great thinkers of the seventeenth and eighteenth centuries who argued that society is held together by an often unspoken or unwritten agreement that the very poor will refrain from revolution if the very rich will allow even a modicum of their wealth to trickle down to the lower levels. Under this sensible agreement the rich pay taxes to ensure domestic tranquillity. Any large movement that imperils the ancient modus vivendi endangers the democracy.

I find it cynical that now both the political right and the religious archconservatives borrow this almost sacred word *contract* to mask their intentions. Instead of meaning, as it did, a high-minded agreement among classes in the eighteenth century, the term now identifies a slick device to fracture the agreement. The results could prove disastrous in the decades ahead. It is for that ominous reason that although I can see merit in some of the provisions of the contracts, I am frightened by the overall impact of the proposals. The noble contract engineered by Samuel Adams, Benjamin Franklin, George Washington, Alexander Hamilton and Thomas Jefferson must be protected and preserved, for from it stems the greatness of our nation.

Having watched at close quarters the operation of several state legislatures, I shiver when I hear that the new Republican agenda includes closing many operations now supervised by knowledgeable men and women in Washington, with the budgets and the responsibilities being shuffled off to the states. I am not heartened by this prospect of allowing fifty different state legislatures to determine what food, if any, should go into the school lunch for deprived children. Nor do I like the scenario of the state legislatures' trying to decide how to discipline fourteen-year-old girls who have had illegitimate babies.

My assessment of state legislatures was accurately voiced by an unnamed comedian when he or she said: 'No man's life, liberty or property is safe while the Legislature is in session.' And a paraphrase of a political cartoon I saw recently exemplifies a dangerous trend that portends ominous consequences for our nation: 'The young colonels want to give the poor back to the states, and all the rest of America to the big corporations.'

Americans forget that our nation has already experimented–unsuccessfully–with a loose confederation of sovereign states not bound by any superior central authority. When the thirteen colonies declared their independence from Great Britain on July 2, 1776 (not July 4, as popularly believed), some form of government was required, and the ineffective Articles of Confederation were instituted and governed our fledgling nation during the years 1781–89. Patriots quickly saw that the Articles were a tooth-less form of government, since the central agency lacked the power to collect taxes from the individual states, enforce tariffs or pay for an army. A movement was launched by the leaders of the thirteen confederated states, and in May 1787 delegates assem-bled in Philadelphia, where they labored until September 1787 on the drafting of the Constitution as we know it today. The first Congress convened in 1789, the birthday of our present govern-ment, and one of its first acts was to begin developing the Bill of Rights.

Government by a loosely bound collection of states was thus tried and it failed, but even so the Confederation did manage to pass a few bills of considerable benefit to the nation as a whole. The laws governing the distribution of national lands were ex-emplary; the rules laid down whereby a territory could graduate into statehood served the nation well in the next hundred years. Nevertheless, the Fathers of our country bade farewell to the Confederation and welcomed with opened arms the establish-ment of a strong central government endowed with extraordi-nary powers, and it is the assaults on that basic concept of government by the young colonels that should be sounding warning bells to us all. Over two hundred years ago America found a form of government ideally suited to the character of the people; let us not at this late date alter or imperil that proven form at the whim of young radicals.

I am personally affected and greatly agitated by one of the stated philosophies of the new young colonels' regime. When its leader said repeatedly, during his battle to win votes for his party, that members of the other party could not be considered to be in the mainstream of American life and that liberals generally could not be trusted to behave like responsible Americans, and when he even questioned the patriotism of Democrats and liberals, his arrows of contempt struck me with ugly force. Was my Americanism truly in question? Was it possible that I was little better than a Communist? Was it right for him to read me out of the mainstream, and was my patriotism faulty?

When I first heard this charge I was taken aback. This political leader of the young colonels in the House of Representatives was speaking of me, and I had to review my record to see where my failure to be a good American lay. When our nation was threatened by Adolf Hitler and the Japanese militarists, I joined the navy even though I could claim exemption from military duty because of my age (thirty-six) and my religion (Quaker). I served two long tours of duty in the South Pacific, and during the Korean War I participated at one time or another with all four branches of our armed forces: army, marines, air force and navy. I went along on patrols probing enemy lines. While serving aboard our great aircraft carriers, I flew as a passenger in our dive-bombers as they operated against Communist rail networks. I survived three airplane crashes, the last in the middle of the Pacific, and when I returned to civilian life I ran five times for political office, lost but was successively appointed to seven major government boards, including the one that supervised NASA and the International Broadcasting Board in Munich, which managed our radio broadcasts to nations behind the iron curtain.

Instead of the Speaker's questioning my patriotism, I think I have a great deal more right to question his—although of draft age, he evaded service in the armed forces. No, I shall give him the benefit of the doubt and alter the word *evaded* to the possibly more gentle *avoided; evaded* carries a sense of his having taken specific steps to escape a duty, and he has explained several times that he was excused under the same legal exemptions that allowed so many other leading Republicans of our generation to remain at home. I accept his excuses. But the fact remains that I went to war and he didn't, and I get angry when he presumes to read me out of the mainstream of American life, as if he were now the sole arbiter determining what behavior is now acceptable in America.

The dangers created by the young colonels are not limited to their revolutionary behavior in the 1995 Congress. They represent a real shift in American attitudes, and I expect to see their Speaker eventually running for the presidency. But if the voters of Virginia were brave enough to reject Colonel Ollie North's bid for the Senate in 1994–and he the beau ideal of the typical young colonel–the nation as a whole might also reject this Speaker for the young colonels.

In an age when we have wisely become aware of some of the weaknesses of our present government, we must also be aware that rash overcorrections could threaten the miracle that the early patriots achieved when they devised our unique system of government. Meeting in Philadelphia during that hot spring and summer of 1787, they were a choice selection of political geniuses. Many had attended colleges in both Europe and the American colonies. They were widely read; they understood the lessons of history and the grim conditions that could engulf a country ruled by tyrants or ambitious kings. When I read of their prolonged debates and discussions concerning what a good government should be, I am amazed by what a wide body of historical reference they drew upon: Greek history, Roman, medieval times and recent events in their European homelands. They were as brilliant a group of men as could have been gathered at that time by any nation of the world.

I have been immensely impressed by the fact that of all the world's governments that were functioning then or thereafter, ours has been the longest-lived and the most successful. All others have been forced or have elected to modify their systems. Great lands like Russia and China have changed spectacularly, while smaller nations like Switzerland and Sweden have altered their forms of government. If some would suggest that Great Britain has existed longer with one unchanging governmental structure than we have, I would point out that the individual states that constitute Britain have undergone striking changes, such as transforming their kings and queens into useful figure-heads and altering enormously the relative powers of the two branches of Parliament, with the House of Lords becoming more or less a figurehead while the Commons really controls the government.

No, we in the United States have the most successful form of government the world has ever known, and since it has proved so worthy and storm-tested, I look with dismay at attempts to alter it overnight by dictate from untried young colonels whose breadth of experience cannot begin to match the philosophical and political wisdom of our Founding Fathers. The victorious young colonels are not free to nullify our social contract and ride roughshod over our historic traditions.

Recommendations

1. Since the young colonels won the election by a huge margin, the nation should pay them respect by studying with care the proposals of their Contract with America and the Contract with the American Family.

2. Those provisions that we find acceptable should be supported, but those that are clearly outside the American tradition should be vigorously opposed.

3. The drift toward turning over to the states functions now performed by the federal government is an invitation to slide backward to the year 1777, when our newborn nation attempted to
govern itself with the ineffectual Articles of Confederation. If a
new Confederation is forced upon us, I predict that within a
decade we will junk it, as before, and return to a strong central
government.

4. We must not be afraid of a reasonable national debt. If we
drive our economic system back to debt zero we will soon regret
it and change the laws to permit a workable debt. Excessive debt
such as we have today should be cut back, but only within reason.

5. As we revise our government we must keep in mind the over-
riding economic problem of how to provide employment of
some kind for those trapped in poverty.

6. I would move with extreme caution in negating the worthy
results of affirmative action. Termination of all such laws will be
interpreted as a kind of declaration of war between the races, and
a nationwide alienation could result with dreadful consequences.

7. A constitutional amendment limiting terms in Congress would
be a mistake.

8. Do not permit a school voucher plan that diverts tax money to
private schools.

9. Do not allow draconian laws to be passed disciplining young
women. Work out some more humane way of dealing with early
pregnancies.

Looking
Ahead

*T*he basic structures of the United States are so firmly rooted that they can absorb the radical changes signaled by the 1994 elections. We have seen that at least half of the twenty alterations proposed by the contracts of the nation's new congressional leaders were sensible and in many cases overdue. They can be installed without danger to the republic.

But I am worried about the other half, for they are the blueprints for a 'leaner, meaner' nation, as if some powerful person swinging a broadax were chopping his way through a leafy grove, indifferent to the harm he was doing and the changes he was making in the landscape.

Leaner, meaner nations do not prosper. They lack the resilience that enables them to adjust to change. They abuse their citizens to the point that rebellion becomes inevitable. They halt the orderly movement of workmen regardless of where they are on the economic ladder, and they bedevil their lands with a cramped vision lacking breadth and inspiration.

I believe that the genius of the United States is basically humanitarian. We are idealists who have always been willing to experiment with new social orders and new solutions to old problems. We are not a horde of people who will march backward in lockstep. We cannot long be satisfied with changes that are mean-spirited and destructive of our less favored citizens.

As I survey the long reach of American history I find us to be a people willing and even eager to help our neighbors. Our school system, which was once such a powerful force in uniting the nation, our willingness to build roads that would join our various districts, the brilliant manner in which we used capital to pay for new factories and workmen to staff them, and the proliferation in all parts of the country of local committees to support hospitals and libraries and symphony orchestras are proof that we are essentially a people with a cooperative spirit.

The current move to demonize liberals, calling into question their validity in American life and even their patriotism, is a dangerous leap in the wrong direction. It goes against the grain of American life and should be stopped. The successful nations are those who have mastered the art of alternating between a conservative government (to rectify errors of excess) and a liberal regime (to initiate bold steps forward). Australia, New Zealand, Great Britain and France demonstrate how this can be done, and we ought to be the leader of that noble contingent which has provided the world with such good government and such rock–like stability. We are now in a period in which the programs of the 1929–94 liberals need retuning, and this will be done, but to turn our backs on our poor, to reverse the clock on justice for African Americans, and to ridicule and kill off our activities in the arts would be to commit grave error.

I believe that the basic strengths of our nation are such that we can survive as a world leader till about the year 2050. Our kinetic power, already in action, will carry us forward for half a century. I doubt we could make enough errors in that time to hinder our forward motion. So I am what you might describe as a near–term optimist.

But I am not so sure about the long term. I have spent my adult life studying the decline of once great powers whose self-indulgent errors condemned them not only to decline but in many cases to extinction. Where is the grandeur of Assyria? Where are the glorious legions of ancient Rome? The far-flung greatness of the British Empire? The grandiose expansion of Mussolini's African empire? Or the grandeur of sixteenth-century Spain and the empires of the Aztecs and the Incas?

The life cycle of empires and individual nations involves genesis, exploration, accomplishment, expansion, then loss of courage, contraction, lost mobility and decline. I have never thought that we were exempt from that rule of destiny; this great and worthy nation that has built a new and better life for millions of citizens will also fade slowly and end as every previous empire has.

I can foresee a time near the end of the next century when Japan, a nation with a homogeneous population and a superior educational system, thrives as a major power, unified and able to make strong decisions, while the United States, with our sectionalism and competing blocs, will have fragmented into many different units bound together uneasily, if at all. This will be the inevitable consequence if we make a host of wrong choices.

Our strategy must be to identify the rot, delay the decline and fortify the underpinning. We can postpone our vanishing from world leadership, but only if we adhere to the basics that made us great. I see many danger signals warning us that if we allow our land to break into two nations—one white, one black and tan—we are going to face catastrophe. If we callously sponsor a government that continues to shower largess on the already rich at the expense of the bottom third of the population, violence is bound to result. If we fail to educate our young people in the skills required to keep our system functioning, we condemn ourselves to a second-class position in the family of nations.

We are not exempt from the universal law of obsolescence, but we have one impressive fact to sustain us: of all the forms of government operating on this earth today, ours is the longest-lived. We are the outstanding success. Going back to 1789, when our democracy was launched, all other forms of government existing at that time and competing with us have experienced revolutions, wild changes, slow decline and a discarding of the form of government they had in that year. Even stable Britain was forced to convert its once powerful monarch into a mere titular head and to change its House of Lords, which had been a coequal partner of the House of Commons, to a ceremonial body with little authority.

We are the survivor whose basic roots were sound to begin with and were carefully nurtured and improved as two centuries passed. Now, with dedication to the principles that made us great, we can at least borrow time. Clear sailing–albeit through increasingly roiled waters–till 2050, then the beginning of twilight. But in the next half century we can light new candles of excellence, protect the ones we already have and gain an extension. I wish I could witness the next years of decision; they should be riveting as we face one crucial choice after another. I hope our genius for doing the right thing will guide us.

Index

ABOUT THE AUTHOR

Universally revered novelist JAMES A. MICHENER was forty before he decided on writing as a career. Prior to that, he had been an outstanding academic, an editor, and a U.S. Navy lieutenant commander in the Pacific theater during World War II. His first book, *Tales of the South Pacific*, won a Pulitzer Prize and became the basis of the award-winning Rodgers and Hammerstein musical *South Pacific*. In the course of the next forty-five years Mr. Michener wrote such monumental bestsellers as *Centennial*, *Hawaii*, *The Source*, *Texas*, *Alaska*, and *Mexico*, and the memoir *The World Is My Home*.

Decorated with America's highest civilian award, the Presidential Medal of Freedom, Mr. Michener has served on the Advisory Council to NASA, holds honorary doctorates in five fields from thirty leading universities, and has received an award from the President's Committee on the Arts and Humanities for his continuing commitment to art in America. He lives in Austin, Texas.

ABOUT THE TYPE

The text of this book was set in Nofret, a typeface designed in 1986 by Gudrun Zapf–von Hesse especially for the Berthold foundry.